CREDIT SYSTEM IN EARLY MEDIEVAL INDIA
(*c.* 650 A.D.—1200 A.D.)

CREDIT SYSTEM IN EARLY MEDIEVAL INDIA

(c. 650 A.D.—1200 A.D.)

ARBIND KUMAR

Commonwealth

The publication of this book has been financially supported by the Indian Council of Historical Research. The responsibility for the facts stated or opinions expressed is entirely of the author and not of the Council.

Credit System in Early Medieval India

ISBN : 81-7169-185-4

Edition : 2019

Published by :
COMMONWEALTH PUBLISHERS (P) LTD.
4831/24, Govind Lane,
Ansari Road, Darya Ganj,
New Delhi - 110002
Ph. : 23272541, 23242541
e-mail : commonwealthpublishers2016@gmail.com

Distributed by :
ARJUN PUBLISHING HOUSE
4831/24, Govind Lane,
Ansari Road, Darya Ganj,
New Delhi - 110002
Ph. : 23272541, 23242541
e-mail : arjunbooks2001@gmail.com

Laser Typesetting by :
Dimple Computers
Delhi

Printed at :
Divine Digital Press
Delhi

Acknowledgements

The subject, dealing with a particular aspect of ancient Indian Economic History has attracted my attention long ago and I have since been working on the subject to arrive at judicious conclusion on the basis of materials collected through various sources. Some of my preceptors have always encouraged me to pursue research work with missionary zeal and I have no hesitation in acknowledging that the present work is essentially an embodiment of their blessings. I am particularly grateful to my Supervisor Dr. Bhawani Sharan Singh, University Professor & Head, Department of History, Gaya College, Gaya whose guidanee and overall vigilance served as the beacon light to me all along with completion of my dissertation. I am also thankful to Dr. U.S. Lal, retired Prof. & Head, Deptt. of History, M.U., Bodh Gaya, Dr. Upendra Thakur, retired Prof. & Head, Deptt. of A.I. & A S., M.U., Dr. Chitranjan Sinha, Prof. & Head, Deptt. of History, M.U., Bodh Gaya, Dr. Uma Shankar Singh, University Professor, Department of History, M.U., Bodh Gaya, Dr. Md. Aquique, Univ. Prof., Deptt. of A.I. & A.S., M.U., Bodh Gaya.

I must acknowledge my profound gratitude to Sri Shankar Dayal Singh, M.P. & former Secretary, Dr. B.N. Pandey, Principal, and teachers of B.D. Evening College, Patna for their inspirations, valuable cooperation and blessings. I have no words to acknowledge my gratefulness to my parents for their ungrudging help and loving care which kept me sustained to complete the work. I would be failing in my duty if I miss to thank my beloved wife Mrs. Anuradha Anand for her loving cooperation and inspiration during the period of work.

My thanks go to the staff of National Library, Calcutta, Bihar Research Society, Patna, Sinha Library, Patna, Patna University Library, Patna, Mannulal Magadh University Library, Bodh Gaya, Seminar Library, Deptt. of History and Deptt. of A.I. & A.S., M.U., Bodh Gaya for providing all possible help and cooperation extended to me during my visit to those places.

—**Arbind Kumar**

Preface

In spite of considerable progress in the field of research in ancient Indian Economic History, credit has not received the attention it deserved. The subject requires to be studied as a whole in its various aspects chronologically as far as practicable in the light of available data. The present work is an attempt to study the credit system in early medieval India from *c.* 650 A.D.-1200 A.D. with its bearing on certain social and economic issues with the help of literary, epigraphic and other sources.

Credit forms a very important basis of economic relations and growth and is guided by customary rules which develop into a legal shape through successive stages in an advancing civilisation. In primitive society based on an economy where food was collected and shared, necessity to borrow and lend for profit was absent. As men advanced to the food-growing stage, some had a surplus which they owned and others had less for their needs. The economic distance slowly widened to promote the reciprocal urge to borrow and lend. The concept of interest originated in delayed return or non-payment. Usury in diverse forms developed with progress of time and growing complexities in socio-economic life. The growth of a sort of exchange economy bred the demand and supply of the articles of necessity and working capital. Small loans paved the way for emergence of the creditor quite early in some ancient civilizations as revealed by the Sumerian and Babylonian seals and tablets (W. Durant, *Our Oriental Heritage*, p. 228). There the temple functioned as the chief supplier of credit. Similar features may have characterised the Indus culture economy about which much still remains unknown. In the Vedic literature there are evidences on the knowledge of debt in India in an early phase of its history. In the post-Vedic period, rules systematising customs and regulating credit relations were formulated to guard the interests of both the creditor and the debtor in a caste based society. Pledge and other securities became imperative later. As centuries rolled on, changes and adjustments in the regulations and actual workings of credit related to social and economic factors e.g. supply, profit, risk etc., were reflected in the *Smrtis*, commentaries and other sources.

In the course of our study it has been felt necessary to refer briefly to social, economic and sometimes political features as a background in dealing with the subject during the period under review. Though periodisation in the strictest sense is not possible in view of the insufficiency and other known defects of some of our sources, we have tried to follow the generally accepted dates for a chronological outline.

The Smrti works of the period under review, to some extent, suffered from a complex of Brahmanical superiority and commentators tried to harmonise tradition with change. Medhatithi came before 900 A.D., Asahaya at about 750 and Visvarupa in the 9th cent. Sections in Matsya, Agni and Padma Puranas belonged to the period ending 900 A.D. and Garuda to the 12th cent. Amara's lexicon is placed in the 8th cent. at the latest. The grammar of Sakatayana, a contemporary of Amoghavarsa, was written in the 9th cent. The same king patronised the mathematician Mahavira. Brahmagupta, who belonged to the Ujjain school, wrote in 628 A.D. His scholiast Prthudaka was later than Bhaskara of 1150 A.D. also of the Ujjain school. Sripati of uncertain date shows the strong interest taken by the Jains in commercial education. Rajasekhara was patronised by Mahendrapala (893-908 A.D.) and Damodara, the author of Kuttanimatam by Jayapida (779-813 A.D.).

The Smrti commentaries and digests blossomed since the 11th cent. Mitaksara composed by Vijnanesvara in 1070-1100 A.D. or 1118-27 A.D. shows an unbiased mind. We have accepted Kane's dates for Kulluka (of Bengal), Aparaka, Laksmidhara, Devanabhatta, Chandesvara and other commentators.

Kalhana wrote in 1050-80. Somadeva wrote Kathasaritsagar in 1063-81. Somadeva who wrote Yasastilaka in 959 was different and a contemporary of Krsna III. Ksemendra of Kashmir of the same century not only reproduced a story literature and Samaya matrka but also Lokaprakasa, a work on the deeds of loan. A similar work from Gujerat was Lekhapaddhati, a medieval compilation, where the loan bonds were all dated V.S. 1288. Vidyapati's Likhanavali, another similar work, was done in the 14th cent. Prabandha Chintamani, Prabandhakosa and Puratana Prabandha Samgraha were of the 14th cent.

Of the late Jain writers Siddharsi worte in 906 and Hemachandra his Dvyasraya in 1088-1172. Halayudha of Bengal and Ksirasvamin figured in the 11th cent. Damodara of the Gahadavala court wrote Uktivyakti Prakarana, a grammatical treatise. The author of Manasollasa was Somesvara III of the 1st half of the 12th cent. Naisadhiya Charita appeared before 1200 and Jalhana's anthology in 1250. The locale of the sources is no less important than their dates with regard to their relevance in particular regions.

Particular care has been taken in utilising epigraphic material on an extensive scale in addition to the literary sources, especially the legal literature, subjected to critical enquiry, while fully acknowledging whatever help I have derived from published writings on different aspects of the subject dealt with. I have referred to *Sukraniti* for a comparative study and not as an ancient text, as it has been ascribed to the 19th cent. by some on important grounds, although Kane attributes it to *c.* 1300 A.D. and M. Gopal uses it for the Maurya age. For the same reason reference has sometimes been made to *Vivadabhangarnava* of Jagannatha of the late 18th cent. as well as to some texts including proverbs and lyrics of uncertain, controversial or very late dates. For purposes of comparative study it sometimes becomes necessary to refer to a tradition and custom which may find a place in a much later work and their relevance in particular contacts is to be judged with caution for what it is worth.

Abbreviations

A.B.	Aitareya Brahmana.
Angu N.	Anguttara Nikaya.
Anta das.	Antagada dasao.
Ap. S.	Apastamba Srauta
Asa	Asahaya.
A.S.S.	Anandasrama Sanskrit Series.
AV.	Atharva Veda.
B.I.	Bibliotheca Indica.
Baudha.	Baudhayana.
Bija.	Bijaganita.
Br.	Brhaspati.
Brahma.	Brahmagupta.
Brhad. U.	Brhadaranyaka Upanisad.
Br. Kalpa.	Brhat Kalpasutra
Br. Katha. ma.	Brhat Katha manjari.
Br. S.(ph). S.(id).	Brahma Sphuta Siddhanta.
Chanda.	Chandesvara.
Chh. B.	Chhandogya Brahmana.
Col. Dig.	Colebrooke's Digest.
Comm.	Commentary.
Comm. Vol.	Commemorative Volume.
D.K.	Dharma Kosa.
Devana.	Devanabhatta.
Digha N.	Digha Nikaya.
di.	dinara.

divn.	division.
Divya.	Divyavadana.
Dra/dram.	dramma.
ed/Ed.	edited.
Fel. Vol.	Felicitation Vol.
G.B.	Gopatha Brahmana.
G.O.S.	Gaekwad Oriental Series.
Gau/Gaut.	Gautama.
Go. Gr. S.	Gobhila Grhya Sutra.
Grad. Say.	Gradual Sayings.
Har.	Harita.
H.O.S.	Harvard Oriental Series.
Ins./insc.	Inscription.
J/Jat.	Jataka.
Jyotisa.	Jyotisatattva varidhi.
K/Karsa.	Karsapana.
Kal.	Kalanju.
Kala.	Kalam.
Kalpa.	Kalpasutra.
Kas.	Kasu.
K.S.	Kathaka Samhita.
Katha S.	Katha saritsagara.
Kat.	Katyayana.
Kau. B.	Kausitaki Brahmana.
Kau. U.	Kausitaki Upanisad.
Kaut.	Kautilya.
Kavya.	Kavyamimamsa.
Krtya.	Krtya Kalpataru.
Kur.	Kuruni.
Kuttani.	Kuttanimatam.
L.P.	Lekha Paddhati.
Likh(a).	Likhanavali.
Lila.	Lilavati.

L. Pr.	Loka Prakasa.
Laksmi.	Laksmidhara.
Lud.	Luders.
Maj. N.	Majjhima Nikaya.
M.B.	Maitrayani Brahmana.
M.S.	Maitrayani Samhita.
M/Man.	Manu.
manj.	manjadi.
Man. Sr. S.	Manava Srauta Sutra.
Ma. Pa.	Madana Parijata.
Ma. Ra	Madana Ratna Pradipa.
Madana-p.	Madanapala.
Madana-s.	Madanasimha.
Mbh.	Mahabharata.
Medha.	Medhatithi.
Mil/Milinda.	Milindapanha.
Mita.	Mitaksara.
Mitra.	Mitramisra.
M.N.U.	Maha Narayana Upanisat.
Mrchchha.	Mrchchhakatika.
Muhurtta.	Muhurtta Chintamani.
nal	nali.
Nanda.	Nanda Pandita.
Nar.	Narada.
N.B.P./NBP	Northern Black Polished.
N.U.	Narayana Upanisat.
Nir.	Nirukta.
N. India	Northern India.
Old and Pis.	Oldenberg and Pischel.
P.	Purana.
Paipp.	Paippalada.
Pan.	Pana.
Pan.	Panini.

Pan. B.	Panchavimsa Brahmana.
Para Ma/ma.	Parasaramadhaviya.
Pinda n.	Pinda niryukti.
Pkt.	Prakrit.
Prab Chin.	Prabandha Chintamani.
Prab. Kosa.	Prabandha Kosa.
Praja.	Prajapati.
Prthvi.	Prthvi Chandra.
P.T.S.	Pali Text Society.
RK.	Rastrakuta.
RV.	Rg Veda.
Rajat.	Rajatarangini.
Ram.	Ramayana.
S.B.	Satapatha Brahmana.
S.B.E.	Sacred Books of the East.
S.B.H.	Sacred Books of the Hindus.
Sad. Pun.	Saddharma Pundarika.
Sak.	Sakatayana.
Samaya.	Samaya Matrka.
Sam. N.	Samyukta Nikaya.
Sankh. A.	Sankhayana Aranyaka.
Sarattha.	Saratthappakasani.
Sa. Vi.	Sarasvati Vilasa.
Skt.	Sanskrit.
Smr. Cha/cha.	Smrti Chandrika.
SV.	Sama Veda.
T.A.	Taittiriya Aranyaka.
T.B.	Taittiriya Brahmana.
Tr./tr.	Translated.
T.S.	Taittiriya Samhita.
Taka.	Takakusu.

Trisasti.	Trisastisalakapurusacharita.
Uktivyakti.	Uktivyaktiprakarana.
Upamiti.	Upamitibhavaprapancha-katha.
Uva. das.	Uvasaga dasao.
V./Vol./vol.	Volume.
V.S.	Vajasaneyi Samhita.
Vachas.	Vachaspati.
Vas.	Vasistha.
Vijnana.	Vijnanesvara.
Vi. Ra/ra.	Vivadaratnakara.
Vis.	Visnu.
Vr.-Har.	Vrddha-Harita.
Vi/vs.	Verse.
Vya. Ma/ma.	Vyavahara Mayukha.
Vya. Pra/pra.	Vyavahara Prakasa.
Y/Yaj/Yajna.	Yajnavalkya.

Contents

1

Socio-Economic Background —Kinds of Loan and Interests —Rates of Interest

(FROM 650 A.D. TO 900 A.D.)

Social and Economic Background

The period from 650 to 900 A.D. is represented by the minor Smrtis like Vyasa, Harita, Prajapati and Bharadvaja, the later Puranas like the Agni, and by the earlier commentaries in Asahaya, Visvarupa and Medhatithi. It thus marks a chapter in the development of Dharmasastra literature.[1]

The period saw resurgence of Sanskrit, Prakrit, Tamil and other literatures in their several branches. In this age of Puranic renaissance[2] which was also the golden age of Tamil Hinduism,[3] the Brahmanas were a dominant minority both in the north and the south and caste restrictions became rigid.[4] Hence an attempt by the commentators to uphold older Smrti tradition and reconcile the anomalies of the Smrti compilers with regard to debt laws among other regulations. But theological superiority could not match the social competence of the major class of people who had been gaining a kind of control over the means of production. The

1. Cf. Age of Imp. Kan., p. 202; also R.S. Sharma, Light etc., p. 136.
2. Age of Imp. Kan., p. XVI.
3. K.A.N. Sastri, Hist. of S. Ind., p. 351.
4. Age of Imp. Kan., p. XIII.

rise of the Sudras had become a factor of growing importance. This was recognised by Medhatithi of about 900 A.D. who denied that a Sudra was a chattel to be enclaved at will or pledged.[5]

Another aspect of this reaction against orthodoxy was women's liberation both in the north and the south which also was acknowledged by Medhatithi as to inheritance, education, administrative rights, immolation etc.[6] Both the aspects might have had a bearing on interpretation of debt regulations with regard to Sudras and women, e.g. in their right to contract debt and mortgage that would be binding on others. We find a stronger trend in the period and after to enlarge the scope of Stridhana,[7] which presumably the husband's creditor could not seize. Even courtesans enjoyed a respectable position in society and treatises on love and pornography came much into vogue.[8] We not only find courtesans and devadasis being socially rehabilitated by marriage[9] and some temple-girls and mistresses of royal personages making endowment[10] side by side with queens, but also fines were to be imposed on merchants favoured with tax exemption if they committed sex offences against minor girls and labour women.[11] This coincided with the ascendancy of the mother-cult and the cult of Yaksinis in many parts of India.[12] There is ample evidence in literature to show that agriculture and industry were fairly operating[13] in a closed economy, though the pattern was everywhere not the same.

5. On M.X. 128; D.R. Chanana, I.J.S.W. XX no. 3, p. 201 f.; Age of Imp. Kan., p. 370.
6. Ib. p. 367 f., XIX.
7. Altekar, Position of Women, 221; R.M. Das, Women in Manu, p. 215 f.
8. Rajas. Kavya X, p. 53.
9. J.I.H., Vol. 43, pt. 2.
10. 114 of 1914—4th yr. of Aditya I a temple prostitutes saving being accepted as a pious endowment.
11. C.I.I. IV no. 32.
12. J.A.S.B. XXII no. 2.
13. Amar II. IX. 78.

Eastern India under the early Pala kings and south India under the early imperial Cholas maintained trade links with South-east and East Asia, but the economic penetration by the Arabs in the west was a significant phenomenon. This caused a further lag in the participation by Indians in Central Asian and Western trade which had already declined because of the rivalry of the Chinese merchants especially in silk trade[14] since the 5th century. The Chinese now rivalled by the Arabs, especially since the conquest of Sindh, preferred the south-east Asian sea-route. Confronted on both sides by foreign competition, North Indian trade suffered. Although we hear of the presence of Indians in the Far East,[15] the brisk spell of Sino-Indian intercourse of the 7th cent. recoiled in the 8th to revive later. There was a drop in the Indian share of East Asian trade over the seas in spite of tariff walls raised against Chinese ships calling at Indian ports.[16] Sea-voyage, fraught with piracy, was disapproved and had little significance to Medhatithi who again lived far off the coastal area, in the determination of interest.[17] Eclipse in trade was reflected in guilds losing good-will and other corporations were in the picture, but village assemblies were preferred for investment of endowments made to temples and monasteries.[18]

The paucity of metalled money deepened, for there was not only a dearth of small coins as in the previous period but also of the higher denominations. The Siladitya coins, the imitation—Gupta and Puri-Kusana pieces, presumably passing at a lower value than their proto-types,[19] as well as the Kasu and silver pon of the south, serving sometimes as a money of account, could not fill the gap. Cattle constituted an important item of wealth,[20] accounting for the numerous cattle-raids as before and for cattle endowments for livestock

14. Ibid.
15. Mahavira Ch. V. Vs. 19.
16. Ind. Hist., 153.
17. L. Gopal, p. 132.
18. L. Gopal, pp. 130-1, Agni, Ch. 254.
19. Causes of decline in guidhood have been analysed in L. Gopal, p. 81.
20. Cf. Dobbins, J.E.S.H.O., Vol. 14, p. 289.

redistribution among villagers especially in the south. Paddy was not only an item of endowment but an established unit of value, as materials to be supplied as interest on perpetual endowments in land, money or gold were calculated in terms of paddy measures. These testify to widespread prevalence of barter side by side with money economy for convenience. Sulaiman refers to shells and small copper in currency.[21] All this led to insistence on security for loans, unredeemed land mortgage, occurrence of payment in kind or by service for want of cash, slavery for debt and imposition of high rate of interest, as well as stricter laws about recovery and liability.

In fact, North India did not revive from the economic depression caused in the last century of Gupta rule. Land grants increased as a result in the post-Gupta period, especially with Harsa in the north and from an earlier time in the south, but heavily from this period. This was characteristic of what is called feudalisation by some scholars.[22] Sharma even observes in assignment of levies on items of trade and manufacture a sign of feudalisation in the industrial sector.[23] Other traits were visible in the rise of self-sufficient rural units of production, setback of urbanisation and weakening of central authority. Affluent cities of old like Pataliputra and Kausambi[24] declined as a result of economic dislocation and political turmoil. The rise of Kanauj at a commercial cross-road to an imperial status like an oasis in desolation was envied by powers all around. The triangular struggle that ensued, not possibly devoid of this kind of economic significance, and also the ferment in the west caused by Arab depredations not only added to the storm and uncertainty but also gave rise to petty feudatory principalities as local centres of strength. Invasions, feudal wars and cattle raids[25] combined

21. E.I.V. 17, p. 310.
22. Renaudot, p. 17.
23. Kosambi, Culture and Civil, 197 f., Myth and Reality, etc. Sharma, Light etc., p. 144 Ind. Feud. etc. R.K. Chaudhuri, J.I.H. 1959, P.I H C 1970), p. 29 etc.
24. Ind Feud., p. 239.
25. Kosambi, Cult. and Civil, p. 196.

with flood[26] and famine[27] to accelerate the forces of chaos. In such a background of greed[28] and laxity of moral scruples, prices fluctuated[29] and capital was bound to be shy. There could be less investment in trade and much less in long-term loans, so that royal initiative and religious sentiment were necessary for a steady flow of capital in the form of perpetual endowments, while a search for fields of safer investments, e.g. in buying and renting enclosures bought with endowment money had come into vogue.[30] Besides lapse or sale of gage-fields, gifts brought about a concentration of land in the hands of a non-cultivating social group, temples, monasteries and institutions of learning[31]—a feudalistic change in the land pattern. In consequence of investment by them in lending mainly for productive purposes, credit became to an extent institutionalised with little opportunity for the common man to get out of plight in respect of consumption loans.

Kinds of Loan

In an economy where commerce was sporadic and a professional class of traders and lenders was not sharply differentiated or fully operative, there could be no commercial credit in proper sense. All loans outside the area of temple operations were but private contracts between the lender and the borrower and most of them were unproductive. In consumption loans the money received would be spent at once or the commodity consumed before long, so that each advance bore the risk of dead loss. These therefore carried high interest and were attended with afflictions of usury. Linked to barter were commodity loans. Prativastu denoted borrowed article in a 7th century Sanskrit Buddhist text.[32] Yachitaka in Matsya Purana had the same sense. Loans of clothes, grains, gold

26. 298 of 1905 (record of a Vaidumba chief).
27. Seminar A.I.H.C. (C.U.) held in 1970.
28. Famine in Kashmir—Rajat, V. 68-121.
29. Kadambari, p. 175.
30. Two records of Pandya Varaguna II show divergences within a span of four years.
31. Ibid.
32. S.I.I. II 574.

and other articles were mostly for consumption, as it appears from Medhatithi on Manu VIII 140. Yet loosely speaking a portion of the commodity loans was linked to commerce, as may be gleaned from certain commentaries. Medhatithi refers to the possibility of growing rich with earnings from the borrowed article by trade or reloaning. His carrying on trade with borrowed money is attested.[33] This seems to have been discouraged by the canonist. In such cases, the debtor does not seem to be a helpless one but often a grain-dealer who posed as the poor producer's debtor deferring payment and thereby depriving him of a due increment. Asahaya on Narada I, 4 and 6 tells a story[34] that a trader Durddhara borrowed a sum of ten thousand drammas from a Brahmin Sridhara for his business at the rate of 2% p.m., i.e. 24% per annum, the trader died after paying the first month's interest 200 drammas and that the great-grandson wanted to plead his inability. Two problems appear in Ganitasara of Mahavira[35] as examples of the rule (VI 54) for arriving at the same capital dealt out at two different rates of interest. Borrowing @6% and then lending a sum @9% one gains 81 in 3 months. The capital to be found out is 900 (VI 55). Borrowed @3% p.m. and put to interest @8% p.m., a capital begets 80 in 2 months. It is found to be 800 (VI 56). Although the second sum shows a much higher difference and reloaning at the exhorbitant rate of 96% (nearly 100%) per annum, the figures here have no literal significance as being only of an exercise in commercial education. However, it shows lending of borrowed money to be quite remunerative. Borrowing of capital for reloaning was definitely a loan with economic purpose. Money, gold, grain and livestock endowments to temples in south India were invested with village bodies and thus in part transformed into agricultural loans and advances. Sometimes cattle obtained in raids and gifts were in this manner redistributed among guilds of cattle-rearers on condition of paying

33. M.S V Vinaya II 127.9, 125.1.
34. Medha on M. VIII 151.
35. Story quoted in Kane III 289 f.n, 395; S.B.E. Vol. 33, p. 43 f n. 6.

interest in kind to the temples. Thus, temples served as a means of binding together court and country in 'politico-economic symbiosis.'[36]

Kinds of Interest

The six kinds of interest mentioned by Brhaspati were known to writers of this age, some under different names. Like Brhaspati Vyasa[37] defines Kayika as interest derived from the body, e.g. milk received from a cow pledged or the service from a beast of burden or manual labour.[38] Another verse ascribed to Vyasa, Kayika is defined in a different sense that is found in Narada. This corresponds to Brhaspati sikha vrddhi or hair-interest that grows on daily. On Narada IV 104, Asahaya[39] explains Kayika as the type of interest which is paid every day at the rate of one pana or a quarter without any diminution of the kaya or dravya i.e. the capital, which has to be paid in full. Medhatithi (M. VIII 153) explains it as repayable by physical labour but does not clearly say whether labour could reduce the capital also. As noticed earlier, the incidence of Kayika was to be observed only among the poorer section and lower orders of the society. Bhogalabha in Brhaspati may be traced in the enjoyment of live pledge under one sense of Kayika[40] above as well as in what is called stoma[41] in Vyasa. If Bhogalabha was concerned more with the use of immovable pledge like house, it was identical with stoma and not Kayika of Vyasa. Stoma in Vyasa probably included satisfaction from actual use besides the enjoyment of rent as specifically stated by Brhaspati and Katyayana. Enjoyment of field sometimes went towards the interest and also reduced the principal if enjoyment more than covered the interest.[42] Such a pledge known to Vyasa as sapratyayabhogyadhi

36. Ch. VI (V) acc. to Mahavira himself as he does not count the first chap. on Samjna, Vs. 55.
37. G. Spencer, I.E.S.H.R. VII no. 4 (1970), p. 434, ib. (1968), p. 292.
38. Vs. quoted in Smr. Cha. II 359.
39. Kane, III 418.
40. Ibid.
41. Ibid.
42. R.C. Nigam, Ind. Adv. VII (1967) III-IV 47.

but if it is argued that Vyasa understood enjoyment by actual possession under adhibhoga (from bhogyadhi), enjoyment of rent under stoma and enjoyment of benefit from live pledge or debtor's person or cattle under Kayika, one may discover a classification of this type of interest (adhibhoga/bhogalabha) made by him. Medhatithi (M. VIII 151) also refers to interest by enjoyment—adhibhogah gobhymyadah.

About periodical interest (Kalika) that is calculated or collected by month, Asahaya states that the rate of interest in this case remains in the traditional 2-5% range according to caste.[43] But here the rate is no point of classification of interest. Even the month as a periodical unit was not always adhered to in calculation, so that Medhatithi remarks that the use of the word masa was only illustrative, the interest not being allowed to remain unpaid beyond a given time, be it a day or a month.[44] Here is an attempt by Medhatithi to accommodate daily interest prevalent in his days within Kalika of Manu—to make it reprehensible in the eye of the law giver. There might have been certain practical bar to accumulation of interest unpaid by way of raising the rate, if any instalment failed.[45]

Medhatithi refers to a custom that may have existed in a particular locality, by which the capital was to get doubled if payment was not made within a time limit.[46] Kalika may be observed in the sums of Mahavira; in some the instalment amounts increased in arithmetical progression, the rate remaining the same.

Asahaya[47] again introduces rate of interest in explaining Karita and describes it as an interest which is offered by a debtor himself in distress at a rate exceeding 10%. Bharuchi[48] and Medhatithi[49] lay stress on settlement of this type of

43. Nar IX 20-21.
44. Ibid.
45. On Nar. I. 103.
46. On Manu, VIII 153.
47. Cf. Chatterji, Op. cit., p. 46.
48. Ibid.
49. On Nar., I 103.

interest in mutual benefit of both the parties. Obviously, Katyayana's pious emphasis on acceptability of Karita to debtor was not observed in practice, for the acuteness of the debtor's need left little scope for his choice of terms, which were almost always dictated by the creditor in Karita. This definitely entailed transgression of the Sastric rates. Medhatithi refers to another type of Karita where gold was issued as loan to receive interest in cloth by stipulation.[50] Here also not the rate but the mode of payment does matter. Presumably, such loans were taken by the weavers individually or in guild or by cloth merchants. These well correspond to endowments in S. Indian epigraphy where gold or money was invested to provide clothes to monks or deities. The dictum of Agni Purana[51] about svakrta vrddhi tallies verbatim with Yajnavalkya (II 38).

Asahaya defines and illustrates chakravrddhi at length : 1 dramma lent can multiply 500 times and the process of compound interest can continue for 33 years 4 months. He adds (on Nar, I 104) that a capital will increase to its double in 20 months @ 5% p.m. to quadruple in 40 and octuple in another 20 months and so on. He assumes that this type of interest implies the transcendence of dvaigunya limit. But here dvaiguna has another significance as it becomes the point of conversion of the capital when interest is allowed to be merged with it to bear further interest. Here interest is to bear interest only when it has become equal to the original sum. In later concept,[52] the conversion period need not tally with the period of doubling at a given rate and it may be a year or a month or as stipulated. In Chakravrddhi according to Bharuchi,[53] the increase was attached to the original like a wheel to the cart, or it revolves like a wheel. In his attempt to explain desakalavyavasthitah in Manu VIII 156, Medhatithi refers to wheel analogy and presents the illustrations, the hiring of a cart and carrying one's burden by bull in which

50. Manu VIII 152-3.
51. Ibid.
52. S.I.I. III no. 128.
53. Ibid.

cases interest is charged only for the period during which each is put to use. If there is a river on the way to cross or the day is bad, in which case the cart or bull becomes useless, no interest should be charged.

This fanciful interpretation makes wheel interest identical with hire-charge of a cart or beast of burden. To explain Medhatithi's analogy, it may be presumed that originally the term was applied to interest charge on loan to caravan traders at a high, special rate. If for some reason there was delay in the caravan's progress, that period perhaps was to be exempted, or if it could not move at all, the special rate was not to be charged. The interest was merged with the capital to bear interest, because the accumulated sum could be rolled into investment to the profit of the traders. Compound interest was sanctioned by law-givers as a punitive measure after renewal of an outstanding debt accumulated to double and as a penalty on the creditor who made adverse use of a pledge. It is noteworthy that there was no sum on compound interest in mathematical texts; the reason perhaps was that it was banned in law and was practised only in informal or clandestine way. The mathematical texts incorporated sum on interest being realised on accumulated interest with no violation of the dvaigunya limit in the first stage of the development of compound interest. The creditor collected an instalment of interest before the expiry of the term to invest it with a different borrower. Illustrations of this have been found earlier in Aryabhata and now in Brahmagupta[54] and Mahavira.[55] The implication of lending the interest to another borrower remaining within dvaiguna and in the next stage relending it to the same borrower is important in the genesis of compound interest traced previously. In the absence of cash, payment of instalment failed only to usher in compound interest, the debtor having had to agree to pay interest on unpaid interest.

Rates of Interest

Rates of interest may be seen in the legal texts and compared with those observed in mathematical works and incriptions.

54. The Universal Encyclop. of Mathematics, p. 262.
55. On M. VIII 152-3 Ref.

Deviations from the Sastric rate of 1/80 of the principal per month (i.e. 15% per year) in this period were acknowledged in special cases. Thus Vr-Har.[56] states that double of the same may be charged in the absence of a pledge or security. Har (qu. by Chanda & Vachas)[57] allowed the principal to get doubled in 50 months at the rate of 8 panas per month for 25 puranas (1 purana=16 panas). It comes to 1/50 per month or 24% per year. In another quotation[58] Har. lays down a pana per purana which amounts to 1/16 part a month or 75% per year. These divergent statements of Har., if none had been interpolated, may be explained as pertaining to different regions or times or according to the nature and extent of security as in Vyasa. From Har.'s statement deduces that a silver raktika equalled forty raktikas of copper, but as the relative value of silver and copper varied depending on supply of silver especially the rates of interest were bound to vary even within the same period. Vyasa[59] agreed with Yaj (II 38), Vr-Har. (IV 226, ib.) and Agni Purana (Ch. 253 v. 62) that 1/80 (15%) was the normal rate on a loan secured by pledge but specified 2% per month (24% a yr.) when money was lent on personal credit and 1/60 (20%) when a surety was offered.

Commentators strained their ingenuity to explain and harmonise the statement of their authors in order to make them relevant in changed circumstances. According to Asahaya 2% was to be charged from honest men only irrespective of their caste.[60] It is interesting to note that caste alone did not matter in extending loans, and even a Brahmin of bad credit would not be entitled to a low rate, whereas a non-Brahmin of establishment credit was. As a matter of fact, the creditor had the final say in judging the bonafides of a debtor at the time of fixation of an interest rate. Consequently 2% rate was becoming inadequate and rare. In order to support 2-5% rates respectively for debtors of four castes in descending order,

56. Brahma XII, 15.
57. Mahavira, Ganitasara, Ch. VI Vs. 45, 46.
58. Asadha, 1370, p. 63 ed.
59. Kane III 420 f.n. 683.
60. Vi-Rs. 11.

which was in excess of the 1/80, Medhatithi[61] presents as a ground the creditor's having been poor with a small capital (alpamdhanam) and unable to maintain a large family (bahu kutumbasya) from $1^1/_4\%$ received or having religious commitments (mahate dharmaya) or having to take great risk when his debtors are not of particularly religious disposition. In short, necessity is adduced as a ground for the increased rate. He adds that when the creditor understands that his capital is going to be invested by the debtor in extensive business, he may charge 5% interest irrespective of caste,[62] but a rate in excess of that would be usurious. This again seems to have been an acknowledgement of the non-observance of caste distinction in reality, though Visvarupa (on Yaj II 38) writes on the grading of interest rate according to caste that was only theoretical.

Rates of interest in non-canonical texts are worthy of note. The Paninian stigma for lending ten to receive eleven (12%) persisted in Sakatayana III 2.30 dasaika dasat thascha (garhye). Different rates also prevailed in Sak III 2.157—udardhat thah, dvitiyo-smin nasmai va vrddhirayo labha upada sulkam va deyam dvitiyikah, trtiyikah, panchamikah, sasthikah, ardhikah. Similarly in Sak III 2.158, bhagyah, bhagikah, ardha and bhaga denoting rupakardhah. Although panchakah, saptakah in III and masikah, samvatsarikah in III 2.102 f. are not stated to have had debt significance as in Panini, it cannot be said that such percentages had become obsolete by the time of Sakatayana in respect of interest.

In mathematical texts, we find sums of interest showing given percentages of interest per month, within a particular range of rates. In Brahmagupta only the rules are stated and the examples are supplied by his commentator Chaturveda Prthudaka Swami. Although the latter belongs to a slightly later period, his examples may be considered in this connection and these are conspicuously similar to the examples given by Mahavira of this age.[63] The sums on Brahma XII 14 & 15 give

61. Kane III 421 f.n. 685.
62. On Nar. I 101.
63. On Manu, VIII 141-2.

3% (twice), 5% (twice) and $12\frac{1}{2}\%$ (once) per month, where 5% rate predominates, as that was also the charge on a silpinyasa. Mahavira himself supplied dozens of interest sums.[64] The rates vary from a little less than 2% ($1\,^{7}/_{8}\%$) to a little more than 13% ($13^{1}/_{3}\%$). Those between 2% and 6% are predominant as pointed out by L. Gopal. At a closer observance it is found that the 5% rate (per month) claims the highest incidence. Although figures in mathematical exercises may not perfectly conform to reality, the repeated occurrence of 5% is perhaps statistically significant. Next come 3% and 2% close at each other but in less by 50% cases than the 5% rate. 4% and near 4% cases are so few that they need not be considered in groups. Taken with the fractions, 2-3% group view with the 5-6% group, the latter being slightly heavier and showing thereby the trend of the rates to get higher with 5% remaining the norm. Considered as a whole, 2-5% group is again statistically significant and tallies with 2-3-4-5% rates prescribed in the legal texts which in reality was not based on the debtor's caste but his solvency and reliability. It is also seen that divergent rates were operative. Reloaning by a creditor in two cases was made at the same and moderate rates, whereas loaning by a borrower was made at the higher rates of 8% and 9%. Payment by instalment seems to have been in vogue, but the sums given here appear merely as mathematical exercises.

Here it may suffice to mention that different rates from 5 to 100 per cent per year were obtained in this period with 20% per year being predominant especially in Pandya and Bana records.

No clue is obtained for all the divergent rates in the epigraph and mathematical texts, and no exact ground can be adduced in specific cases particularly of the kind stated in the Dharmasastras, except that they were linked to shifts in the broad pattern of economy, especially money supply, prices of articles, credit needs and high or low credit. Divergence of rates may sometimes be attributed to the nature of loan purposes. Extra rate was permissible in commercial credit.

64. On Manu, VIII 152.

Medhatithi was aware that 5% was chargeable in case the borrowed money was going to be put to extensive commercial use (Manu VIII 152). On Manu VII 157, he says that the verdict of experts in trade by journeying, for which sea-voyage stands by illustration only, will be final in determining whether compound or stipulated interest was chargeable on a loan according as its investment will be profitable in a particular distant country. This implies that sea-voyage fraught with piracy had little significance to Indian traders who engaged in coastal trade only by this time,[65] far less to a writer of North Indian interior. The prohibitive Kautilyan rates on sea loans is met with in Agni,[66] which reiterates 20% per month (i.e. 240% yearly) on loans to sea traders and 10% (i.e. 120% yearly) on loans for trading in distant villages instead of through forests, the latter being particularly relevant to a closed economy of the village.[67] This high premium was put in consideration of the risk to the loan as well as the wide margin of profit expected. But as no other sources of the period allude to special rate for bottomry loan, the incidence of these rates may be said to have been very low.

Differential rates depending on caste of the debtor in the scale 2-3-4-5% was made conditional by Medha.[68] This could be charged only when the creditor was unable to support his large family on taking $1^1/4$%, had a small capital, had religious commitment or when his borrower was not righteous. It may be supposed that even if the commentator intended each of the additional conditions to be present, in practice any of them could be adduced as an excuse of charging high rates. The additional conditions were not considered sufficient for taking more than 2% from a Brahmin. A Brahmin along with debtors of the other castes could be charged 5% without distinction when it was understood that the money would be put to profitable venture (on Manu VIII 152). That is to

65. Ch. VI.
66. Ibid.
67. Gopal, p. 131; p. 145.
68. Vs. 65, Ch. 253.

say, in commercial credit even the Sastrakaras as understood by the scholiasts did not allow any caste distinction in matters of rate. Had the discriminatory rates been therefore introduced for consumption loans only? But some of the loans to Vaisyas, the agricultural, industrial and trading community (to bear 4%), were of productive and commercial nature. To them this increase in rate was not considerable as in the case of a Brahmana or Ksatriya who invested borrowed money, while it made no difference to a Sudra in similar circumstances. Perhaps the law-makers could not afford to further alienate the Sudra who was in the production relations more than a Vaisya was. Asahaya reflected this phenomenon when he wrote that an honest and solvent Sudra did not have to pay more, which is compatible with the rise of the Sudras. We should remember that the entire outlook of these writers was framed in Brahminical complex and what really mattered in charging low rate was not high caste but high credit depending on economic solvency and social status. Besides, it would become impossible for a poor Brahmin to get loans at the lowest rate, and excuses to whitewash the high rates for him would be invented by Brahmin writers to induce the lender to meet his credit need. The most convenient way out was the Karita interest. What is important, we do not come across any such caste-based rates in the mathematical examples or in the epigraphs.

If again, interest rates were profit-based and risk-adjusted as they are bound to be by economic pulls,—there would be considerable variation according to rates and amounts of profits earned, and too much fluctuation in the interest rates, individual bargaining and money-lenders' devices for transgression would render prescribed norms merely pedantic.

It is almost certain that the rates recorded in endowments were lower than the market rates to allow a margin for the capital being re-invested by a guild or village assembly. In fact, the real investor was not the donor but the temple or monastery who would receive the interest in kind. As they were not professional lenders, or rather in the absence of professional lender who would agree to lend in broader interest, they would lend money, gold, cattle or grain at moderate

mostly as a prop to national economy. It is possible, though evidence to that effect exists for the next period, that monasteries and temples would generally make advances to followers of respective sects, not only to favour the devotees but also to attract prospective converts, and in this preferential treatment some discriminatory rates might be existing. But no differential treatment in the matter of interest rates is met with in the investment of 1400 Kasy by Pandya Varaguna II[69] in the same year at the uniform rate of 20% with 16 bodies of which many were sabhai or Brahmin village assemblies, some ur or non-Brahminical assemblies and a negarattar or town corporation. No special rate for caste was allowed, belying the Sastric rule.

Differential rates may be guessed from an epigraphic record between investment with a religious purpose and that with a mundane objective. This is by no means certain, for the demand for paddy might have sharply increased by this time, or again the purpose not stated might have been other than secular.

Differential rates with regard to maximum accumulation of commodity loans are prescribed by writers of this period too with certain deviations. Bharadvaja[70] sanctions double on gold, 3 times on grain, 4 times on cotton cloth and silk cocoon (or silk by upalaksana) and base metals like copper and 8 times on ghee and sandalwood and 6 times on oil and the offspring on a female animal loaned. It is difficult to agree with his scholiast (Sa. Vi. 229-30) who advises to take kosa to stand for paddy and karpasa for rice etc. in upalaksana. Kosa is silk-worm that may stand for silk, while dhanya has been separately mentioned. Vyasa[71] recommends 9 times on edible plants, cotton or seed and sugarcane and 8 fold interest on oil, juice, spirituous liquor (madya and asava) if kept for long. Vrddha-Harita[72] prescribes 4 times on cloth, 3 times on grain and 2 times on gold and Harita[73] 2 times on tula,

69. Kaut. III 2.1.
70. Manu, VIII 142; Har in Col. Dig. I.45.
71. E.I. XXI 101 f.
72. L. Joshi, D.K.I. I pt. 2.
73. Ibid.

the significance of which is not clear, and 3 times on paddy, wool and cotton. His scholiasts Chandesvara and Misaru Misra think that double was allowed on paddy if repaid in two or three months from the next harvest, but it was to increase 3 times if paid in a year (also applicable to wool and cotton), and that the author sanctioned 8 fold increase in a year on ghee, salt and raw sugar. They were probably reflecting conditions of their own age, but the 8 fold increase on other items, which tallies with the evidence of other writers of this age, does not follow from the text. Commenting on above Sharma says that the principal was likely to be realised in addition to this, but the return was always considered inclusive of the principal—when a capital was to become double, the increase would be 100%. Medhatithi permits the special rates on grain, fruits, beasts of burden and wool and quotes[74] (or misquotes?) a passage ascribing its content to Narada and Yajnavalkya to say that those writers permitted 2 times, 3 times and 4 times on gold, cloth and grain. In fact, the two authorities cited agree on permitting 3 times on grain and 2 times on cloth (Nar. I 107, Yaj. II. 38). Anyway, Medha had no objection to 4 times on grain and 3 times on cloth ordinarily, which might be pertaining to his time and place, if he meant the purport of his quotation. He allowed 5 times on grain if only the lender found himself in distress, the debtor thriving on the borrowed grain.[75] He also tried to link the 5% rate in a saving clause which may imply that successful venture with borrowed capital was a remote possibility (Manu VIII 152). High rates were dependent on a debtor's success with the loan.[76] There are two verses apparently inconsistent with each other in Agni Purana[77] on different rates. In Ch. 254 Vs. 17, offspring for female animal, double for grain, quadruple for cloth and octuple for juice are stated. Ch. 253 Vs. 64 writes double on gold, treble on grain and quadruple on cloth; the first half-verse not satisfactorily translated by

74. Ibid.
75. Visnudharmottara Purana X. III. 331. 18-19.
76. On M. VIII 151.
77. Ibid.

M.N. Dutt[78]—"a seventieth part of its original value increased seven or eight times (i.e. 7/70 or 8/70?) will be the charge on any female animal pledged"—admits of restoration. Sasantati in the other verse itself confirms our point that "saptatistu" in Vs. 64 Ch. 253 should be restored as "santatistu" and "saptasya" as "sattvasya to mean extract as "rasam" in the other. Double on dhanya also is not appropriate to this age. Pitamaha states 5 fold increase on rupya or base metal including silver and 8 fold on land. On both the points he agrees with Katyayana (512) who however uses the term Kupya that excludes silver. It is possible that silver became more scarce in the days of Pitamaha. In case of land, 8 fold return might mean eight times the produce at one harvest. But what interest would the debtor have in cultivating a borrowed land with all expenses to give away the full harvest for at least 4 years (taking two harvests a year) especially when the loan period was not definitely stated? More probably the interest in case of land would be 8 times a particular quantity of grain depending on its area and yield. Otherwise one has to believe that the law-givers and lenders took it for granted that the borrower would take recourse to fraudulent practices to satisfy both himself and his creditor according to the Sastric rate of 8 times the harvest or land-value. Lend-lease of land was an innovation from the late Gupta period and inscriptions show house-sites being leased by temples. Probably, the owners found it difficult or unprofitable to cultivate lands under direct supervision and agreed to lend land as a form of subinfeudation. Men of the cultivating class, who probably lost their tillage or had been ousted from hearth and home, might have prayed for loan of land[79] or rather the loan of tillage right, but the issue is highly controversial.

It may be observed that the rates on utility goods were higher than on gold, silk or precious objects, grains being an exception 100% on gold etc. in comparison to 800% on juice, oil or salt does not indicate that the yellow metal was more available. But lowering of rates on the utility goods than in

78. Age of Imp. Kan., p. 406.
79. Ch. 253, Vs. 64.

the previous period may indicate greater availability and vice versa, though there might be other reasons. Six times on oil with Bharadvaja or 5 times on fruits with Medhatithi marked this change. Base metal that was to increase 5 times perhaps became available with 4 times increase, but silver became scarcer and registered a sharp rise from 2 to 5 times in rate accounting for the lack of silver currency. The rate on gold remaining steady with all the writers recorded a stable position of the metal;[80] linked to it were the price levels of grain, cloth and liquids enjoying stability in certain parts of the country. Three times on grain remained the usual rate, barring Medhatithi of this period and Brhaspati of the last (4 times). The stability of cloth and silk garments was due not so much to internal factors as to the steady supply of woven stuff from China,[81] so that the 4-time rate on cloth was unhindered by 6-time rate on its raw material (cotton) known to Vyasa and by 5 times and 4 times on silk cocoons[82] to Brhaspati and Bharadvaja respectively. No change has been marked on seed sugar-cane from Br. to Vyasa or on sandalwood from Brhaspati to Bharadvaja; the supply position probably remaining the same. Being of south Indian origin, Mahavira presents sums on sandalwood pieces (V. Vs. 7,42), horses (ib. Vs. 39), cocoanuts, slaves etc. (strewn all over). Medhatithi writing on royal monopolies on Manu VIII 399 refers to silk and wool of the east, horse of the west, pearls of the south[83] etc. He refers to urna called lava in the north (Kashmir?—on Manu VIII 151). The superfine cotton fabric of Rahma (Pala kingdom ?) was also known to Sulaiman.

80. Tr. Agni Purana, p. 910.
81. Sharma, Light etc. p. 129.
82. E.I. XX. p. 99.
83. Ganitasara, Ch. V-Vs. 19-300.

2

Security–Pledge–Mortgage–Recovery

(FROM 650 A.D. TO 900 A.D.)

Security

It has been discussed in chapter I of this work that different rates of interest were prescribed as loans were accrued or not in Agni, Vyasa and Vr-Har. on a pledge loan, the rate was 15% but in absence of security the rate was 24% in Hariti and others and 30% in Vr-Har. It is Vyasa who first prescribes different rates according to the nature of security—1/80 per month or 15% per year, on a loan secured by pledge and 1/60 per month or 20% per year when there is a lagnaka or surety.[1] Obviously, a pledge offered greater security than the personal credit of a debtor and the guarantee of surety taken together.

Hariti[2] mentions different forms of security as proofs of legal value. In a suit a loan does not stand without an adhi or a surety or a bandhaka or a witness or a document. This is identical with the verse of Brhaspati (X. 5) except in sequence. If Brhaspati's advice was in the descending order of acceptability to a creditor, it was in the ascending order of legal validity that Hariti mentions securities, the two orders almost coinciding. If however law as known to Hariti placed greater reliance on factual proof than documentary evidence, then it may be said that Hariti proceeded on a descending scale of legal safety. Unlike Brhaspati he mentions lagnaka before bandhaka and witness before document.

1. Ibid.
2. Ibid.

Of different forms, the pledge was obviously the most effective security. Likewise its sanctity or inviolability was a matter of concern for the depositor. Utmost care was required for the upkeep of a pledge as of a deposit, which was sometimes called nuasa. The irksome obligation in looking after a nyasa lest there be a sthanabhramsa is mentioned in Kuttani.[3] Nyasa niksepa and upanidhi were rather loosely applied to deposit.[4] Visva (on Yaj. II 69) makes a distinction and defines nyasa as an open deposit in safe custody and niksepa as an article delivered to one for being handed over to another. Agni Purana states that the custodian who derives any benefit from an aupanidhika dravya or harasses the depositor or fails to return it except on ground of its loss by accident, robbery or subversion of government, was liable to refund twice as much its value. Agni Purana (Ch. 227, Vs. 8.10) and Matsya Purana brand one who refuses to part with a deposit and one who makes a false claim of deposit as thieves, the fine being equal to the value of niksepa. Vyasa describes the reasons why a niksepa is placed by the owner[5] and sanction punishment for one who misappropriates it. He also grades the compensation according to the nature of the causes of non-return. The custodian was obliged to return the same (value) if it was lost or damaged through accident or royal disfavour while being retained after it had been asked back. An amount less than the value was to be paid if it was lost through inadvertence, but its full value with an interest[6] was to be paid if it was consumed by the custodian. On this point the affinity between a deposit and a pledge is the strongest. At this stage the depositary becomes a debtor in respect of the used up bailment. If the custodian makes earnings from the deposit by investing it in lending or so without the permission of the depositor, he was liable to pay the value with an interest[7] and also a fine to the king. If the deposit is held up, it will be repayable at one and half the value but will increase 3 times in 3 months

3. Vs. 455.
4. Amara II ix. 81.
5. Ibid.
6. L. Joshi D.K. I, p. 2.
7. Agni Ch. 254.

and after that this amount will increase at compound interest. Incidentally, compound interest was thus acknowledged as a penal measure. A deposit becomes a pledge as soon as anything is drawn upon it by the depositor.

Pledge

Asahaya[9] understands adhi to be a transference of authority (short of full ownership) over a thing put as security. Vyasa accepts the broad division of pledge into movable and immovable.[10] Bharadvaja and Marichi know of four kinds of pledge: bhogyadhi, gopyadhi, pratyayadhi and ajnadhi—of which the last two are new.

In pratyayadhi,[11] the pledge is to be enjoyed to the extent and during the period as stipulated, neither more nor less (by implication). This is probably the point of distinction from bhogyadhi which is not to be enjoyed more than recorded; but here over-enjoyment is forbidden and not the shortage in enjoyment.[12] In such cases presumably early redemption does not matter but there are circumstances as in the case of a milch cow pledged or a field where early redemption is detrimental to the interest of the pledgees that a time is fixed for redemption for all practical purposes. Probably, pratyayadhi covers this type of time-bound pledge. Shortage in enjoyment of pratyayadhi is to be compensated for during debt settlement, while if enjoyment exceeds the stipulated interest, the debtor is to be paid for the margin.[13] By implication, in bhogyadhi, enjoyment beyond the interest was to be counted in repayment but the debtor was not obliged to satisfy the creditor during settlement if the latter reaped less benefit than expected to cover the interest. Thus, in fact, pratyayadhi was a kind of bhogyadhi or rather the two were slightly different forms of usufructuary mortgage. Income from a pledge in excess of interest might be due to an

8. Vyasa.
9. Nar. IV. 124.
10. Ibid.
11. Ibid.
12. Ibid.
13. Ibid.

increase in its value. But no consideration seems to have been made of the increase in value which might be due to the pledgee's contribution. Ajnadhi[14] seems to be a pledge registered by king's order in court. Dr. Chatterjee[15] takes it to mean a pledge ordered by the king or the court to be presented. A bhogyadhi which is properly recorded in royal office before being deposited[16] is best. This is necessary to avoid future dispute as to its condition before bailment.

Gopyadhi is a thing pledged to other but kept with oneself. This is hypothecation. Another type of pledge for custody, according to Asa, is kept with adhipala type of surety which is handed over to the pledgor when the debt is paid up and is a variety of Har's krtakalapaneya. According to Pitamaha, a time bound pledge placed with an adhipala surety is delivered to the creditor if a debt is not paid. Again, Vyasa probably meant by gopyadhi that kind of pledge which lapsed with the accumulation of interest to double, for he advises that it should be released after the capital gets doubled.[17] Har says that a pledge should be returned as it had been received and according to terms as recorded.[18] According to Vyasa,[19] gopyadhi was to be kept in creditor's custody and not to be used by him, so that interest would accumulate. Vr-Har rightly points out that field and garden are kept as usufruct and things of daily use may be placed for custody only.[20] For whereas non-use of such things as utensils saves them from depreciation, with no risk of deterioration as such a field cannot remain uncultivated with any of the parties. Agni[21] adds that gopyadhi will cease to take interest if used like a sopakara where interest is reaped by enjoyment and is to be restored if lost except by accident or royal disfavour.

14. Vr-Har.
15. Op. cit., p. 218.
16. Ibid.
17. Agni P.
18. Ibid.
18. Ibid.
19. Balkrishna, Op. cit., p. 294.
20. Ibid.
21. Ibid.

Like Yajna, Agni asserts that Kalakrtam is lost with the expiry of the term, but phalabhogya does not perish (Vs. 18). Rules enjoin the pledgee to acquire the bailment.[22] If during placement he does enjoy a bhogyadhi, he not only hence loses his right to enjoy but also the increase of his wealth.[23] If he does not get possession of adhi the debtor should be made either to hand it over or return the money to the creditor.[24] In any obstruction is made by debtor to his taking possession, the debtor is to be punished with six times the value of pledge and forced to allow its enjoyment.[25] Vyasa and Har too agree on pledgee's non-liability if loss is due to causes beyond his control. But if it is lost owing to his fault, he is to pay its full value but the debt with interest is also payable to him.[26]

The misappropriator incurs his own ruin. The creditor is not entitled to get back his money so long as he holds up a pledge, the debtor also does not get it back till both settle to mutual satisfaction.[27] If the pledge is lost for no fault of the pledgee, the debtor, according to Vyasa who agrees with Brhaspati and Katyayana, should either replace the pledge or pay up the debt.[28] Even if it deteriorates in value in spite of proper care, it is to be made good. According to Haritis even a part of the loan should not remain unsecured. If more is taken by debtor promising to make good the pledge-value, that must be delivered to the creditor. In Kuttanimatam perhaps an example of this is furnished. A courtesan is said to have placed a collar of pearls with a merchant through her maid and received 30 kedaras and wanted more, while she had taken comphor, sandal, saffron, incense etc. from time to time. When approached by the creditor she advised him to keep the necklace as his property at whatever price set up on it by a mediator and promised to pay the balance if any within a few

22. Agni, Ch. 254, Vs. 20.
23. Vyasa.
24. Ibid.
25. Ibid.
26. Ibid.
27. Ibid.
28. Ibid.

days.[29] Haritis[30] asserts that in case of loss of a precious pledge by fault, the creditor loses his principal only, if the pledge be of equal value, and incurs the payment of the entire value of the pledge, if it be double of the amount lent (presumably deducting his loan dues). Taken in the light of the statement quoted above (f.n. 89), he is to pay the excess only; that is to say, he pays the pledge-value minus the principal which he has already paid and the interest that is his own, both remaining in the hands of the debtor. We thus differ from the rendering made by Chatterjee[31] in accordance with the interpretation of the scholiast. It is rendered that the loss of the pledge would lead to the loss of the principal and the pledge is lost to the creditor because he cannot claim another pledge. He adds that the pledgee should lose an amount equal to the value of the pledge (Smr. Ch. II 328). Loss of pledge of equal value and loss of pledge of double value cannot be met with the same penalty—loss of principal. The scholiast's explanation of the creditor's loss of pledge as because another pledge is not to be provided is not acceptable. If the principal is lost, no question of replacing a pledge does arise, and there is no meaning in stating that here. It must mean compensation for the pledge, for it is unwise to suggest that the debtor should loose the pledge-value above the principal in his hand for no fault of his own. The scholiast corrects himself saying that adhinasa means that the creditor has to part with an amount equal to pledge-value. If that went to the debtor entirely over and above the creditor's loss of the principal, he would be loser and the debtor would be gainer to the extent of the principal, again an imbalance, which a law-giver would hardly intend. In fact, the pledgee's responsibility for the loss would go to the extent of the value of the thing inclusive of the capital forfeited. We are to take dhanam nastam (i.e. the first part of the result) in the text to apply to tatsamo which comes first and the second part dhanikasyadhir to dvigunam that follows tatsamo. Such a sequence to convey

29. Vs. 605-6091; Vs. 609.
30. Ibid.
31. Ib. p. 270.

a sense is often met with in Sanskrit, though ambiguity is apt to create confusion. Besides, Har passes the onus of paying for the spoilt pledge on to the surety in case he was rich and the pledgee impoverished.

On adverse possession of a pledge by pledgee, Medhatithi tries to harmonise vs. 144 and 150 in Manu VIII, stating that in case the pledgee did it perforce against express disapproval of the pledgor.[32] the penalty is the loss of entire interest, but if he does it secretly and the pledge is not destroyed (except for the loss of brightness in gold etc.) the result is loss of half of interest.[33] Medhatithi attributes to Yajnavalkya[34] the opinion that where a pledgee uses pledge by permission of pledgor's servant through whom the pledge was placed but pledgor at a later stage cancels the pledge, the loss would be half the interest. He disputes it saying that as the servant had the authority to give that permission, the possession cannot be regarded as adverse. According to him, possession without the permission of a pledgor of an unredeemed pledge after the loan has become double is not a serious offence. By implication, this is to result in loss of half-interest. This question of ownership may be discussed under redemption and lapse below. Medha adds that loss of entire interest as a punitive measure for forcible enjoyment applies to cases where interest exceeded the value of enjoyment.[35] Where pledgees like ordinary clothes are damaged through use, the debtor should be satisfied by payment of price, but interest will not be lost. In case of precious garments and ornaments damaged by use, he understands both loss of interest and ornaments of price from principal.[36] Yama recommends stern measures against forcible enjoyment and premature foreclosure (by either of the parties), each of which entails a fine of 3 times the pledge-value,[37] besides the loss of respective

32. M. VIII 150.
33. Ibid.
34. Chatterji, p. 267.
35. On M. VIII 144.
36. On M. VIII 150.
37. Ibid.

rights. Even where foreclosure is imminent, any loss caused to the pledgor at pledgee's fault before foreclosure has to be compensated for and if not paid the amount is to run compound interest.[38]

Agni Purana reiterates Yajna's reference to satyankara and charitra bandhaka types of pledge which in any case are not pledge but high personal credit. To take them in the sense of pledge of lesser value pertains to Vijnanesvara of later age. About the divisions of bhogyadhi Vyasa[39] offers two important varieties not known well before; these were sapratyaya-bhogyadhi and apratyaya-bhogyadhi. In fact, the two were subdivisions of pratyaya-bhogyadhi as the authors themselves have distinguished between bhogyadhi and pratyayadhi. The usufructuary pledge in which the benefit was stipulated to be in satisfaction of the interest accrued as well as a part or whole of the principal was called sapratyaya bhogyadhi or pratyayadhi proper. The enjoyment up to a point accounted for the interest and above that for the principal. Vyasa adds that this pratyayadhi is redeemable when loan becomes double. The time of enjoyment of the mortgage is thus adjusted to the increase of the loan to double. In apratyaya-bhogyadhi the income is derived in lieu of the interest money. Sapratyaya-bhogyadhi reminds one of ksayadhi of Yajna. The pratyayadhi, which Bharadvaja[40] explains as the type where the income cf a pledge exceeding the interest is to be returned to the debtor and where the income falling short of the interest stipulated is to be made good, is definitely the apratyaya type of Vyasa. The enjoyment in excess of the principal would not reduce the same. In fact, he does not speak of the sapratyaya type explained by Vyasa, though Kane ascribes the classification to both Vyasa and Bharadvaja. His rendering of Bharadvaja's passage is far from accurate, "if a portion of the principal remains unpaid the debtor has to repay it,"[41] for the term Vrddhi is twice used in the text with the express sense of interest.

38. Ibid.
39. Ibid.
40. Ibid.
41. Kane III, 430.

Chatterjee[42] supposes that apratyaya may be retained by the pledgee for an unlimited period till the capital is paid, because as a kind of pratyayadhi its enjoyment must be limited by the stipulated period and interest. It rather conforms to the Kalika of Agni Purana and to that kind of Krtakalapaneya which Asahaya explains as a pledge that eannot be redeemed within a specified period. However, Vyasa's apratyaya bhogyadhi suggests that there was attempt to bring down the period of enjoyment by a time limit even where the income cannot be calculated beforehand as it fluctuates depending on seasonal conditions, unrealisation, low yield or overuse. Hence the provision for adjustment at the time of release. Medhatithi[43] refers to custom in certain territories existing against the Sastric norm. The enjoyment of an article remains unmolested, "even if the total amount of debt accruing becomes double of the price of that article and the total from the very beginning is paid in gold." Vyasa[44] as quoted by Nanda Pandita holds that a beneficial pledge if time-bound may be redeemed at the end of the term by payment of the principal only but the capital and the remaining interest have to be paid if it is redeemed earlier. Brhaspati (S.B.E. vol. 33, p. 325—Vs. 32-33) shows greater practical sense in this respect. Medhatithi also treats pledges enjoyable at certain periods only. No creditor would like to get his enjoyment interrupted by an untimely release of the pledge as in the case of a milch cow or a field on the eve of harvest. For gopyadhi which is redeemable with interest after the doubling of capital, Vyasa[45] ailows a grace period of two weeks like Brhaspati after which it belongs to the creditor.

By implication, the creditor acquires full ownership after the grace period when he can refuse redemption. Medhatithi belongs to the school of jurists who hold an opposite view.

42. Chatterji, p. 231.

43. On M. VIII 3, tr. by G.N. Jha.

44. Ibid.

45. Smr. Ch. 141.

The question of creditor's ownership over the pledge which is closely linked to one's right to transfer has vexed the minds of the jurists. The pledgee never does seem to hold full ownership. He wields the power of possession of enjoyment while he holds a thing as pledge short of the power to sell or mortgage and this enjoyment is to continue till the doubling point is reached, when he should be prepared to release. Medhatithi however suggests that usufructuary pledge at this stage should remain with him, enjoyment having ceased, till the debtor comes to redeem.[46] It appears that the creditor according to him should wait for an indefinite time. His saving clauses are that only when the creditor has become impoverished possessing only that loan asset and after he has waited sufficiently long (the period is not mentioned) and after he has informed the king, he may sell the gage and is entitled only to the sum equal to double of his loan capital out of the sale proceeds and must transfer the balance if any to the debtor through a third man.[47] The necessity of this act being authorised by the king proves that the creditor does not automatically acquire the right to transfer by virtue of lapse. Medha advises that a pledge should not be long left after maturity as there is every chance of its being misappropriated.[48] It is not stated whether the same rule about gopyadhi was exactly applicable if the pledge was lost during the period or in the grace period. Agni (254/Vs. 22) says that while right of redemption extinguishes with doubling of capital, right of foreclosure does not arise if enjoyment of an usufruct continues. If the creditor is absent (if the reading is prayojakesati) or in the presence of the creditor who refuses to release (if it is prayojakasati), the adhi may be obtained by keeping the money with another family.[49] Restored as prayojanesati dhani for the sake of va in the next verse, it means—"if there be need, the creditor may acquire the pledge kept with another, or it may stay there, its present value being fixed and interest

46. On M. VIII 143.
47. Ibid.
48. On M. VIII 145.
49. Agni P. Tr. p. 914.

having ceased till it may be sold out before witnesses even in the absence of the debtor" (Vs. 22-3). Vr-Har.[50] also agrees that a thing placed with a third person does not yield further interest. The fixation of value by the neutral person is also mentioned in Kuttani (Vs. 455). About foreclosure Yama has to say that it is extinguished by continued enjoyment.

Mortgage

An inscription[51] of his period records a case of temple land having been mortgaged by the priests and then redeemed by paying an amount in paddy and gold. Either he redeemed the land "to make (it) his own" to take the passage literally or redeemed it for the temple.

Submortgage according to Kane[52] was a late development and rules were relaxed to accommodate it by pulls of rising demand for capital.[53] While Asahaya does not take nisarga in Narada in this sense, Medhatithi takes nisarga forbidden by Manu (VIII 143) as a transfer to be understood in the context as a mortgage by pledgee. Medhatithi[54] speaks tolerantly of submortgage by pledgee with the consent of the debtor to realise his money. This he calls purusantara sancharcah. The new loan was to start at a point when the original loan had already increased. That meant that the interest so far accrued was merged to make a new capital, i.e. interest upon interest, transgressing the dvaigunya limit. It meant no extra benefit for the first pledgee. Bharadvaja forbids submortgage if unauthorised by the owner. According to him, if a pledgee does mortgage it even in distress, he shall be deprived of his own money. But he did not have really to lose anything thereby. It does not appear that this subpledge was to be invalid. Evidently the pledge was to be redeemed by the original pledgor from the subpledgee. It is not clear what would follow if the first pledgee received greater sum from his creditor (i.e. the subpledgee) than what would be due to him from his

50. Ibid., IV. 232.
51. Triplicane Ins. of Pallave Dantivarman, 1.4-9.
52. Ib. III 429.
53. L. Gopal, p. 167.
54. On M. VIII 151.

debtor (i.e. the original pledgor). Acceptance of the same pledge for a greater sum is not ruled out, for its value may have increased subsequently. The original debtor would not naturally be held responsible for the excess sum to his new creditor. The latter was therefore to realise his money from two persons according to respective shares in the principal. That the pledge was to be redeemed by the owner from the subpledgee follows from what Prajapati says: "if the creditor subpledges a thing to another for the same amount he shall cause a fresh deed of gage to be handed over with the original one to his creditor.[55] Probably, he is speaking of a submortgage made within the knowledge of the owner, but its application to one made without his approval is not ruled out. The emphasis on the same amount is significant. There is hardly anything illegal in transferring the pledge-right short of full ownership per se by a pledgee for the same amount even against the will of the owner. Handing over the original gage-deed is important, for that forms the legal basis of the first pledgee's authority to transfer by subpledge and also the document by which the subpledgee is entitled to recover his money from the owner. By this the pledgee does not transfer any ownership attribute which he does not possess. One thing irregular about it would be that the owner could have no choice about the new creditor at whose custody his property was to remain. This would be far less serious than a depositary's pledging a thing or lending a sum placed in his trust. For this being done without any instruction from the depositor, Vyasa[56] lays down that the depositary was to bear this as a debt on interest, besides a fine. But subpledge has another aspect. A pledgee obtains money on the security of the pledge from some other creditor clandestinely and invests this sum in short term loan so that it can be recovered before his first debtor should want to redeem. It gives him extra profit meanwhile. But as clandestine subpledge is forbidden in the Sastras no clear reference is made to such

55. Ibid.
56. Ibid.

practices, though this is comparable with lending of borrowed money.

A debtor may want to remortgage a pledge before redemption to get more loan on the same bailment which he may expect when its value has risen but the first pledgee is wont or unable to advance further sums. This gives rise to a question of being within rights to do so and a conflict of possessions. Legally, a pledge that secures by its full value one loan cannot be placed as a security for another at the same time, but this may not be true of a pledge of greater value or of increased value. The debtor may pledge this excess value to another. Remortgage for this extra security and income that a pledge can provide might be true of the usufructuary type of pledge also. But clandestine remortgage was not possible in case of a usufructuary type or a pledge for custody. Mortgaging of a gopyadhi that is kept with debtor as hypothecated contravenes his contract with the bonafide creditor. Bharadvaja[57] on this says that a debtor who forcibly or by suppressing an act of mortgage sells a pledge is liable to a fine of 3 times its value and remains a mortgage in respect of that. A fraudulent transfer naturally becomes void. Otherwise there is nothing illegal in selling a mortgaged property within the knowledge of the parties concerned, for in this case he is selling his ownership subject to the contract of mortgage to a third man. It has been alluded to by Medhatithi as a practice of digressing dvaigunya rule (on Manu VIII 151). Ownership restricted by debtorship may also be transferred in all fairness, in which case the pledgee only loses a choice about his new debtor. Agni (253/52), Brhad-Yama and Vr-Har agree that in sale, gift and mortgage, transference which is first made is the stronger. This applied to remortgaging as well as sale of a mortgaged property. Medhatithi appears to lay emphasis on document rather than on possession in a conflict of transaction. He[58] comments that when a land placed as a pledge to one is again mortgaged to another, the rule that confines the right of the second mortgaged by virtue of his possession for

57. Ibid.
58. On M. VIII 148.

a considerable period (20 years) in spite of the priority of the former transaction and posterity of the latter is not proper. Admitting that a pledge assumes force only by its acceptance by the pledgee which is proved by possession even for a small period upon a thing like land which is always enjoyable while some other things like an infertile cow are not enjoyable. Medhatithi takes pledgee's desire to enjoy as sufficient mark of acceptance. If he has to be away on business or the like he should get the pledge on return even if it has been long enjoyed by the remortgage by dint of his nearness or other opportuities. If one converts a fallow land to a cultivated field, he should get something in respect of the tillage.[59]

In the mortgage of land, cattle and slave which had become a common practice, the expenses the pledgee would have to bear must have been taken into account in the calculation of interest. Pledging of slave women was frequent.[60] The system of live mortgage probably developed from the custom of paying Kayika interest by allowing the creditor to employ debtor's cattle and servants occasionally in satisfaction of interest. Kayika was widely prevalent in the centuries following the Gupta rule amid paucity of coins,[61] and it was not always by working himself but employing his men or beasts that a debtor paid the interest. Employing these for an uninterrupted period and keeping them in the creditor's custody made this phenomenon widely prevalent. Medha[62] however is against gifting and mortgaging of a Sudra. He asserts that slavery is not inherent or perpetual in a Sudra. This dictum was evidently linked with the social forces at work in his time.

The next important security, surety was known as lagnakah and pratibhuvah in Amarasimha, (II, X, 44). Har[63] uses them as synonyms and mentions five classes: Sureties for peace or safety, for honesty or confidence, for payment, for

59. Ibid.
60. Medha on M. VIII 149.
61 Sharma, p. 133.
62. On M. VIII 415.
63. Qu. by Chatterji, 146 f.n. 3.

handing over the pledge to the creditor and for appearance. Each of these types was known to one or other writer of the earlier period, Upasthama in Nar. (I 118) has been taken by Asa in a different sense, that of appearance—a surety to be furnished by a debtor when sued by creditor. It is not likely, as Chatterji thinks it to be, that the meaning of the term remained unclear to the digest writers, for they belonged to the same age. Rather the task of presenting the unwilling creditor and the debtor, as the case might be, got linked up with the release or delivery of pledge. Visva refers to Brhaspati describing debtor as Upasthapya. According to Medhatithi (On Manu VIII 60), avastha was the same kind of pratibhu. If the sense of delivery of pledge to creditor was unknown to Asa or Visva, it very soon developed in this age. For Vyasa makes a clear reference to it where he enumerates seven kinds of sureties. The three new types mentioned by Vyasa are for document, in ordeal and for delivery of a pledge to the debtor,[64] besides the common types dana, pratyaya and darsana. Harita directs that when pledge made in trust is not received by the creditor, the adhipala surety becomes responsible to see that it is handed over to him, failing which he must pay the debt. He was thus a parallel of the surety for confidence who undertakes to pay the creditor. According to Pitamaha[65] in Smr. Cha. in this connection, the adhipala surety in whose charge a pledge has been placed as stipulated for a given period undertakes to deliver it to the creditor, it is not made over by the debtor after that period. From taih samarpanam one may guess that there might be more than one adhipala for the same pledge. Harita[66] also believes in the obligation of a lagnaka to compensate a debtor for the pledge which has been consumed by a creditor; or to pay the creditor if khadaka means debtor. The reading 'syadeko' instead of 'khadako' may mean the debtor as the poor person. The element of compulsion is almost absent, as he presents two provisions, the creditor or the debtor as the case might be has

64. Vyasa, p. 146.
65. Ibid.
66. In qu. L. Josi.

to be impoverished and the surety wealthy. The surety was not to pay any interest on the price. It may be that according to Harita this was a less compulsory aspect of the same surety of the upasthana or adhipala type so that he did not include this type in his list. Probably, for one pledge one or more sureties wielded different kinds of responsibilities known to the writers in the same person or persons, instead of there being a good number of sureties each representing a type and holding a particular responsibility. Agani[67] almost repeats Yaj (II 55) about payment of unpaid debt by several sureties, according to their respective shares of responsibility, but as their responsibility were joint and several, the creditor could sue any one of them. Harita warns a creditor that extorting twice or thrice the amount from a surety will be met by forfeiture and fine.[68] Agni asserts that if a surety is openly made to pay by a creditor a debtor will have to pay double to the surety but no time-limit for this payment to surety is mentioned by earlier authorities. Asahaya[69] writes (Nar I 128) that two or three danapratibhus are held responsible for a loan jointly or according to shares. Visva makes him responsible for the amount proved to be due.[70]

Medhatithi explains niradistadhana (Manu, VIII 162) as a surety who accepts from the debtor for having had to pay the creditor and alamdhana as one who has received sufficient wealth for having to pay up debt. This does not appear to have been a price for the surety's credit. It was a caution money with which the surety would be able to pacify the creditor for a while and recover the rest from the debtor to pay the debt in full. Its amount was to rise in case a debt was large as with the alamdhana type, but how would it be possible for a debtor to deposit an amount with surety to cover his entire debt? The surety for confidence, according to Asa, was to testify to the veracity of the debtor's statements about amounts or instalments so far paid. Surety for ordeal

67. Ibid.
68. Ibid.
69. Ibid.
70. On Yaj. II, 55.

has the obligations to make the debtor go through the procedure or to stand for his appearance when the performance was to take place after some time, according to Chatterji, as suggested by akrte before divye. But akrte seems to apply to lekhye to mean non-existence or non-registration of a document. In fact, ordeal was to be undergone in the last resort. The surety for document was to testify to the genuineness or true import of the deed, being perhaps its custodian too. His role in that case borders on that of a witness to a document.

The surety and the witness,[71] who have to take trouble for others, should neither be self-styled nor made by coercion. It strikes one why person would be willing to stand a surety with all hazards and liabilities. Although the Sastrakaras desired that he should be pious, a surety might become a party to the game of exploitation of the debtor in collusion with the usurer, e.g. by helping in recovery for a share in the spoils by means of seizing chattels. It is not heard that he received any money from the creditor for standing as guarantor. Either the creditor pleased him by underhand means, or the onus of obliging him was skilfully passed on to the debtor whose urge to borrow was greater than the other's desire to lend. It is possible also that he earned a profit from the security money or might enjoy the adhi with or without debtor's permission as a price for his guarantee. In other words, he might sell his personal credit. A surety's obligation was limited. A bankrupt debtor was obliged to repay by service; but in case he was both incapable and infirm and the surety not in a position to pay, it would be too much to expect that the surety should be asked to serve to pay off. He has to pay, if he is able, when the creditor has consumed a pledge. No Sastrakara ever wants a creditor to pay the value of a lost or consumed pledge by service in the last resort, when he has virtually become a debtor to his former debtor.

Witness is different from surety in that he takes no responsibility to pay unpaid debt. Har's mention of saksi before lekhya may not be taken to express his greater reliance on witness than on bond. But importance of witness is great

71. Medha. Ch. M. VIII 169.

when there is no document, e.g. in cases of niksepa generally as it appears from Vyasa.[72] Hearsay evidence of witness is of little legal value to Medhatithi (Manu VIII 74). Vyasa does not insist on number of witness and considers deposition of an honest witness sufficient to establish a case. He also says that alleged defects of witness have to be proved giving no chance to multiplying such allegation (on after-thought). According to Sankha and Likhita, (Vya, Pra. P. 124), physical signs only raise a probability of falseness. Medha is of opinion that women are competent to depose as witnesses where a woman is involved as a party against a man.[73] This proves the rise in women's status in the eye of law. According to Visva (on Yaj. II 71), nice distinctions about many kinds of witness were made only for the sake of exposition and for the understanding of simple persons. Names[74] of more than one witness are recorded in an epigraphic endowment, priests and monks acting as such.

Letters of credit were commonly known as lekhya and also as apakrti.[75] In Kuttani, the merchant-creditor informs the courtesan that whatever money and commodities had been taken by her maid upon the deposit of necklace, from time to time was exactly recorded in the account books (preserved in a casket?) which he wants to present in detail.[76] In Mula-Sar. Vin. text reference is made to deeds and contracts. If they were payable at once, the money or thing was to be realised and distributed, and if not, the deed was to be kept in the treasury.[77] This has been adopted verbatim by Itsing.[78]

Marichi lays great stress on document and advises that a deed should be executed in sale, mortgage, gift or partition of immovable property as it enables one to establish a case.[79] Medhatithi says, where doubt is raised by defective document,

72. Ibid
73. On M. VIII 68.
74. Kanheri Ins IA. XIII 133 f.
75. Ibid.
76. Ibid.
77. Tr. E.P. Mathers, Eastern Leve V.I., p. 75.
78. Gilgit M.S. III pt. 2-ed. Dutt, p. 143.
79. Taka, pp. 190-2.

e.g. made by unworthy persons or that has gradually become illegible, possession for a period confirms its validity. A deed forcibly caused to be made out of greed is declared invalid.[80] In his remark on non-liability of son with regard to certain types of unpaid sum, Medhatithi[81] seems to refer to the practice of a letter of credit in the absence of ready money. A person promises to pay another through a merchant and sends a messenger to convey this to the merchant for whose absence or some other reason the payment cannot be made. No mention is made of any security like pledge or insignia like ring of the Jataka story to inspire confidence in the merchant. L. Gopal thinks that the reference suggests "free circulation of money through letters of credit". Although hundi operates in cash gap, payment by promise relaid through messenger cannot be apt in a closed economy. It is not without significance that this type of unpaid sum was classed by Medhatithi with vrthadanam parihasadinimittam pratisravanam for which son was not liable. A son cannot be relieved of a father's unpaid loan with economic or commercial purpose.

Both Praja and the unnamed author of Smrti Samgraha divided documents in two broad classes—rajakiya or royal and janapada or popular. Praja applied the name sasana to royal charters and chiraka to deeds of debt etc. Chiraka as a kind of janapada deeds was written by hereditary scribes in the capital bearing signatures of parties and names and descriptions of witnesses according to Samgrahakara. Vyasa knew eight kinds of documents—chiraka (spelt with a short i), upagata (receipt for debt payment), svahasta (self-written), adhipatra (pledge deed), etc. Spelt thus Chiraka means a deed written by scribes of the king with permanent validity while chiraka might be derived from bark of tree which might have been its writing medium.

The dvaigunya rule of ancient times for maximum accumulation was no longer being observed. Harita of course holds that after the principal has doubled in 4 years and 2 months @ 8

80. Ibid.
81. On M. VIII 148.

panas for 25 puranas (i.e. 2% p.m.) does not further increase. Bharuchi says that one may take interest up to the equal amount of the principal, be it in a year at a large rate or beyond a year, and that according to some one cannot take interest beyond a year even at smaller rates (e.g. 2%). Different attempts of Medhatithi to interpret the verse shows that the rule was not being observed. He[82] informs that in some countries transgression of dvaiguna are practised by diverse methods. For instance grains are lent in spring to receive double in autumn and sometimes a mortgaged article is enjoyed even after the value of the benefit has equalled the original loan and although the entire capital in gold has been paid. Bharuchi as reported by Medhatithi[83] refers to purusantara-samkramana, by which a capital is transferred to a third person after it has reached double with a debtor. Further interest may thus be charged for the additional period within rules, this being treated as a fresh loan. Medhatithi refers to other methods of transgressing the dvaigunya rule by purusantarasan charah. A pledge-loan before reaching double is transferred to another debtor to start interest from that date.[84] Again when a creditor wants to further invest his money after it has reached double with a debtor but the latter needs it urgently they effect renewal of the deed to evade the dvaigunya principle known as karana parivrtti (on M. VIII 155). By another practice, the debtor takes a further loan from the creditor and before going on travel transfers the same or rather the former loan to a third person.[85] These processes of transference and renewal in its stead to cross the doubling limit were known to Rju or Bharuchi who does not support taking interest above the double from a debt except on renewal purusantarama samkrante punahkriyaprayojanam. It appears that in another convenient way akin to renewal the debtor and creditor could settle the matter, creditor advancing further loan by a fresh document out of which the old debt

82. On M. VIII 168.
83. On M. VIII 159.
84. M. VIII 3.
85. M. VIII 151.

was to be paid up. In a renewal document the interest that has equalled the principal is to be compounded with it to make a new capital and interest thereon according to Medhatithi[86] was to grow at a rate lesser than before, so that it may not be oppressive. The debtor at this time should state clearly the amounts of the principal and the interest before witness. According to Yajva (Bharuchi?), Asahaya and others, reports Medhatithi, a token sum was to be paid this time to enable the witness to see actual transaction. Money neglected for more than ten years would be lost to the owner. Praja also says that a deed should be changed by paying the interest or a part thereof or even a fragment of the principal according to capacity.[87] In a sloke by unknown author capitalisation of interest (mulatvena likhed vrddhim) is advised in a change of deed. The maximum was thus raised with the connivance of the jurists and compound interest enhanced itself firmly. For unpaid debt of an incapable debtor Yama also recommends a fresh deed by compound interest and in case of a usufruct pledge where interest is by enjoyment an additional interest has to be paid with capital. He does not say anything about the rate of the interest and nature of this additional interest. Here then there is no compounding of interest for it has been paid through enjoyment, and as there can be no further enjoyment, separate interest was to grow on the same sum from the point when the debt was to be paid and if non-payment occurs again, compounding of interest would take place at this stage probably. Asahaya[88] says, 1 dramma can multiply to 500 times at compound interest in $3^1/_3$ years, which shows that even the time limit set faded away, though the figures used here were by way of illustration only. This is indicated also by rules in Brahmagupta. The rule in Brahma XII 14, which is about finding the time when a given sum by earning a given interest in a particular time (i.e. at a particular rate of interest) will rise to a multiple of itself,[89] indicates that double

86 Ibid.
87. Ibid.
88. On M. III 155.
89. Ibid.

was not the maximum multiple in every case. In an example furnished by his commentator,[90] the given sum was raised to its triple at 2% p.m. The answer $66^1/_3$ m. also crosses the yearly limit. In the second example,[91] the sum of 20 panas yields 5 in 2 months (i.e. $2\frac{1}{2}$ pana or $12\frac{1}{2}$% in a month) becomes sesquialterate in 4 months—should become $2\frac{1}{2}$ times or 50 in a year.

In exceptional circumstances no interest was to grow on a principal as in famine, political turmoil, religious work and distress, and only the principal was to be paid. This evidently refers to the recurrent crises in early medieval times;[92] it was an attempt to save the principal sums already invested from sinking in the midst of chaos. In crisis period no lender would like therefore to invest in lending. Probably by distress countrywide disturbance caused by invasion or upheaval was meant, for no money-lender would renounce interest in the distressed condition of a debtor. It is also not understandable how a loan incurred for religious purposes could be free of interest in reality. It does not appear to have been a custom observed, for this would encourage wilful non-payment providing an excuse thereto.

According to Vyasa, no interest was to accrue on surety debt, loan secured by usufruct pledge (also refers to pledge for custody being used), a sum offered but not actually received (meaning also a part of the promised loan remaining in the hand of the creditor), nor on fine and duties promised by a submissive person.[93] We prefer to take sulka in its sense of royal dues from its association with fine and not bride price[94] or nuptial gift.[95] Cessation of interest was also to take place on debt offered but not accepted in repayment. A creditor might sometimes like to defer repayment to get more interest when there is little scope for him to invest otherwise.

90. D.K. I., pt. 2, 625.
91. Sharma ed. Vol. I 185 f.
92. Sharma ed. III 776.
93. Ibid.
94. Sharma Light etc. 140.
95 Smri. Ch. II 366.

Sambarta[96] forbids interest on stridhana, profit, deposit remaining as it is, in a doubtful case and on surety debt and if it is not stipulated or agreed upon by debtor. Stridhana refers to deposit of a woman's personal property with husband or any other protector or loan taken from it by the latter, otherwise why the employment by a woman of her stridhana in lending should not fetch interest is not understandable, and Chatterji's remark[97] that "no interest is to be charged on wife's personal property (by the wife-depositor)" has to be understood in this light.

About a friendship loan Asahaya (on Nar 1109) says that if it is not paid when demanded, interest may grow even before six months have elapsed @ 5% per month. Surety debt has been freed from interest on the implicit ground that the surety happens to be a friend. Though it is not stated that it was to be treated as a loan on friendship in which case interest was to accrue on it at a given stage,[98] it seems that it was subject to some such guard against non-payment by surety for an indefinite period. Surety debt does not seem to exclude the interest portion of the amount payable by debtor for it is nowhere stated that a surety's responsibility lays to the extent of the principal only. It does not appear that the debtor's debt to the surety after the latter has paid up comes under the purview of surety-debt.

According to Harita, if pledge is lost for lack of care (and is not restored), the principal is forfeited. Bharadvaja has stated the penalty for sub-mortgaging without owner's permission to be loss of principal. Rules about forfeiture were balanced by warnings of religious demerit and legal action against wilful non-payment. Vyasa says, if an ascetic or agnihotri should die in debt, the merit of his penance of fire worship will belong to the creditor.[99]

By implication, there would be no loss of merit if the debt was paid up by a son or heir, if any, who was liable to pay.

96. Chatterji, p. 67.
97. Balkrishna, Ibid., p. 294.
98. Ibid.
99. Ibid., p. 67.

Padma Purana mentions certain incurable diseases said to come upon a defaulter who does not pay out of greed[100] and says that in the next life the creditor is born as one of his nearest kinsmen to create constant trouble and drainage.[101]

Recovery

In spite of religious blackmail, default and abscension existed, so much so that the authorities of this period while condemning usury empowered the creditor to realise the money by traditional means. Rather he is given a latitude in safe recovery. Bhrgu's dictum that a debtor may be dragged before an assemblage of people and restrained until he pays up according to custom of the country reminds one of the same in Katyayana.

The dharma method is equated by Asa (Nar I 122) with sama of Kaut. Medhatithi[102] explains dharma as agreement to pay at easy instalments. He refers to the method of recovery by stratagem, e.g. by taking ornaments on the pretext of festivity. About distraint and sale of a debtor's articles by creditors, Bharadvaja[103] indicates the order of priority—viz. grain, gold, iron, cattle, clothes, land, slaves and vehicles, in the absence of field his garden and lastly his house and in the absence of even that time should be granted to debtors of three higher castes. Chatterji prefers to ignore the order of priority in sale of articles, but the mention of the immovables and especially the house in the last resort, cannot be overlooked. Bharuchi and Medhatithi interpret acharita as a customary method of fasting on debtor's door.[104] Asahaya[105] refers to fasting not only by creditor but also by his sons and servants (making sons or servants fast would be of little avail). Employment of slaves in the strike could be of sufficient nuisance

100. Interest was to start after a year at 2-5% automatically, Visnudharmottara III 331.7.
101. Nar I, 90.
102. Bhumi kanda ch. XII i.10.
103. Ib-Ch. XV ii.17.
104. On M. VIII 49.
105. Ibid.

value. According to Jolly,[106] if the suitor was to be a Brahmin priest for safety. Medha's discussion[107] of the upayas shows a new approach and indicates that bala or the method of applying force by creditor was not among the recommended means. There it stands for approach to the king who was to apply force. As Vyavahara may mean approach to the king, it is said that from its applicability when other means fail, bala is to be taken in this sense. He refers to the view of Usana who takes bala in the sense of svagrha sambandhi dhanadi as per prakrtinam balam raja as not applicable. According to Chatterji,[108] Medha seems to have been inspired to equate bala with rajasamavesanam from his understanding of a vague passage of Bharuchi, where bala is described as restraining a debtor in creditor's house and reminding him of the consequences of bringing the matter to king's notice.

If binding was not within bala, according to Bharuchi what else it could have been? Besides, Medhatithi does not refer to Bharuchi in this connection, nor does he write about physical pressure caused by the creditor. Medhatithi seems to accept an interpretation which ascribes the methods to the king himself as these occur in the chapter on royal duties.[109] When a debt is admitted or established in court the king is to make the debtor pay by applying any of the means (force in the last resort) and except where there is no want of money pay not all at once but in a manner as not to cause distress in his family. A creditor who applied any of the means himself without informing the king is not punished, however (on Manu VIII 176). Asahaya remarks that these methods are equivalent to one or other of the samadi methods of Kautilya acharita being an extra here. He makes vyavahara an equivalent of bheda to mean a threat of bringing the matter to court But bheda in Kautilya is the diplomacy of discard. According to Medhatithi in vyavahara fresh advances were suggested to enable the debtor to invest in agriculture or trade

106. On M. VIII 49.
107. On Nar I, 122.
108. Rich & Sitt; tr. p. 316; Hopkins, J.A.O.S. XXI 146 f.
109. On Manu VIII 49.

and pay up the debt out of the profit. This was like taking water out of the ear by dropping more in.[110]

Insolvency does not exempt a debtor from paying debt, it is to be realised by making him work.[111] But if the debtor be of higher caste or more qualified he should be allowed to pay slowly and gradually. Thus to Medhatithi possession of good traits and not merely caste superiority is worth consideration. What he says about recovery from a Brahmin is also said about all debtors (no caste being mentioned).[112] He also refers to Narada to say that an incapable Brahmin is not to be put under pressure implying perhaps that a solvent Brahmin might be pressurised.[113] Medhatithi disapproves the custom existing in certain places of a debtor selling himself to pay off as debt could be paid by work.[114] A ksatriya debtor might sell himself to a ksatriya or Brahmana to pay off a Vaisya whom he could not serve.

When a yachitaka or borrowed article is not returned in the same condition, the borrower is to be chastised and made to pay or fined by first amercement instead of physical punishment.[115] Fruitless litigation is discouraged. For a debt denied but established in court a fine is imposed on the debtor. Whereas Manu made the fine 10% (VIII 139), Medhatithi[116] is in favour of considerably reducing it according to means where the debtor is extremely poor or genuinely forgets the transaction (on Manu VIII 51). Agni Purana[117] states the king's share to be 10% from the debtor and 5% from the creditor when the payment is made through court. This appears to be improper, for if the creditor would thus have to lose a portion to the king for no fault of his he would seldom take recourse to law. A creditor applying the means of recovery for a debt admitted is not to be censured and such

110. Ibid.
111. On M. VIII 49.
112. On M. VIII 177.
113. Manu, VIII 49.
114. On M. VIII 177.
115. On Manu, VIII 46.
116. Ibid.
117. Ibid.

a debtor is discouraged from going to court by his having to pay a fine over and above his debt [118] According to Medhatithi this fine, 25% according to (Manu VIII 176), was to be realised not at the cost of the creditor's due (though he applied means of recovery without informing the king). The fine or the king's share was not always the same. According to Yama,[119] when the debtor possesses wealth but does not pay out of wickedness, he is to be made to pay the sum, twice as much being taken by the king. Similarly, according to Vyasa,[120] when the creditor brings a false suit, he is to pay twice the amount in question to the king. In the example of debt suit presented by Asahaya (on Nar I 6), the bonafide of a pleader was called into question to refute his point and the charge of having been bribed was levelled against Durdhara. From the story it appears that pleaders usually were Brahmanas conversant with Smrti literature. The story smacks of litigious spirit instigated by one such. Imprisonment for debt may be known from Sak.[121]

Asahaya explains Nar's rule about accepting part payment, failing which creditor remains liable to pay interest on such sums received and restoration of bond or giving a receipt if bond is lost at the time of final settlement. Nirapakrti in Har may refer to receipt in acquittal.

A debtor having transactions with several creditors is known from Ganitasara (Vs. 49-50, Ch. VI). As to priority in payment, Bharadvaja[122] writes that if one owes several debts to creditors, one secured by pledge and one on personal security, the latter should be paid first and the pledge is to be redeemed after that. It follows that in case such debts are to different creditors, unsecured debts are payable first, and then the secured ones. In the Kautilya fashion, Agni Purana makes debts to a Brahmana and king payable in the first instance, naming the Brahmana before king unlike Kautilya,

118. Ibid.
119. M.N. Dutta, p. 910.
120. Ibid.
121. Ibid.
122. Sak. I. 3.155.

Praja[123] holds that in the absence of kinsmen, the debt should be paid to Brahmanas or thrown into water or fire; thus cast it goes towards one's merit in the next world. The M.S.V. Vin text[124] reproduced by Itsing[125] shows that the loan assets of a deceased monk were to be realised by the monastery and devoted to the use of the assembly. Wrought and unwrought gold, silver and other goods, cowrie shells and coins are to be divided into three portions—for the Buddha, the Dharma and the Samgha.

123. Ibid.
124. Ibid.
125. Ibid.

3

Liability–Usury–Endowment–Donors

(FROM 650 A.D. TO 900 A.D.)

Liability

Sankha repeats the old saying that a son is born to free the father from debt to manes Vr. Har (VII 250-1) and Agni Purana (254/5) reiterate the responsibility of son and grandson or any other person inheriting the property of a deceased person in respect to debt payment. According to Pita[1] undivided sons should pay paternal or maternal debts. In the absence of undivided sons, those who are divided should pay but none was to pay the sum promised by the parent. It may follow that if one out of several sons becomes separate and the rest remain in the joint family, the undivided sons are liable for parental debt and not the separate one. But the latter's responsibility should remain to the extent of his share received in property. Harita[2] however treats a promise made to pay something for religious purpose as a debt during lifetime and after. Vyasa[3] directs that a grandson should pay grandfather's debt and a son should pay the surety debt of father but without interest, while their sons are not liable for the respective debts.

Thus a grandson was not liable for grandfather's surety debt. Son's liability for surety debt was in case of the payment

1. *On Manu*, VIII. 166.
2. *Ibid*.
3. *Ibid*.

surety only and not of other sureties. Vyasa[4] makes it clear that for debt incurred by sureties of confidence, document, ordeal and appearance, they and not their sons are responsible; but sons of sureties of payment and suit should pay unpaid sums. The same is borne out by Agni Purana.[5] The sons of sureties for appearance or confidence were not liable for a sum. We cannot accept Dutt's interpretation that surety's son was never responsible but the parties who had induced the creditor or the mortgagee to advance such sum. Vr. Har[6] has a line that may mean surety debt of mother or father's surety debt in respect of women. The Bengali translation therein suffers from misunderstanding, for the first half verse should go with the second half of the previous verse (Vs. 243) to make a clear sense that if a pratibhu was made to pay twice the sum was payable to him and an equal sum to the king. Sons are held responsible by Agni to pay even debts by fraudulent mortgage of their father,[7] the son and grandson of a person who stood witness to a fraudulent transaction are held responsible for the incidental obligations, according to Agni. This was true also when father or grandfather became mendicant or had great afflictions according to Agni or lived abroad or in distress according to Vr. Har (Vs. 214). A son who lives on his own assets was not bound to pay. Agni exempts son from paying father's debts for immoral debts. Vyasa exempts the son from royal duties, fine or a part thereof or the thing out of contract left by father (also Vr. Har 240). According to Asa (Nar. 144) great grandson (Mulikachaturtha) was responsible for the ancestral debt, though the story he presents (in Nar. 16) shows difference of opinion already current in his days. Jolly comments in his note[8] that Asa here presents his personal view making the textual passage conform to it. Kane[9] tries to refute Jolly on the point of responsibility

4. *SBE*, 33, p. 44.
5. *Ibid.*
6. *Ibid.*
7. Bk II. Ch. IX. Vs. 4.
8. *SBE*, 33, p. 44 f.n.6.
9. *Ibid.*, III. 444.

which according to the latter did not descend to the great-grandson.

With the expansion of the concept of stridhana, conjugal liability for debt needed clarification. A wife stands liable to pay debt incurred by husband if she has approved or contracted it jointly or has contracted it of her own but her co-wife need not pay, according to Agni.[10] Asa (Nar. I 19) and Medha (M VIII 362, IV 214) comment on certain classes of people including actors among whom the husbands share the income of their wives, some even prostituting then, in which case they become liable for wives' debts. Vr. Har makes a wife's second husband (Yosidgrahah—Vs. 242 ib) liable for the debt incurred by her first. Asa takes uttama (in Nar. I. 24) to mean one possessing good fortune and qualities among all svairinis and punarbhus in whose case the second husband would pay the carryovers. Jolly rightly calls this interpretation "highly artificial" for uttama was a particular type of punarbhu, while antima was a kind of svairini. Medhatithi writes that a debt incurred by brother or uncle in the interest of the family should be one even after separation or on return from abroad.[11] This was true also of a debt contracted by servant (grhabhrtya) only when it was in the interest of family and the master was absent.[12]

Usury

A change in the attitude to usury may be observed. Sak[13] may seem to breathe in the Paninian tradition of disparaging usury when he writes on applying 'that in' dispraise (garhye) to form the word Kusidika. But from what he says in explanation it does not follow that he had any hatred for a kusidika who used to lend money on interest. There is no reference to objectionable exaction. Amara[14] also explains kusida as living on interest and makes it synonymous with lending money.

10. *Ibid.*
11. *On Manu*, VIII 166.
12. *Ibid.* VIII 167.
13. III 2.29.
14. Bk II Ch. IX Vs. 4.

Medhatithi writes on taking interest beyond sastric norms but there he qualifies his statement saying that there may be special reason for taking more or beyond the caste rates, e.g. when the money is going to be invested in a highly profitable enterprise.[15] He says that a rich usurer (adhya) should persuade a reluctant person in the wake of spending to accept a loan, but though the creditor thus thrives should not himself be forced to lend.[16] The usurer was known to Amara[17] as Kusidika, Vardhusikah or Vardhsih, who lived on interest. He was of the Vaisya caste as indicated by its mention under Vaisya Varga of Amara (II. IX. 3). However, the creditor in Asa's story on Nar I 6 was a merchant of the Brahmana caste named Sridhara. The examples in Sak may indicate that usury was practised by women too, cf. Kusidaki (III 2 29), also dasaikadasika, dasaikadasiki.

Kuttani[18] alludes to a man who had lost his fortune through the exactions of a usurer. In another verse[19] it is said that a usurer who writes 10 per 100 or ten times 100 (the amount lent) out of cleverness brings about his own ruin; this probably refers to fraudulent deed made by a usurer. L. Gopal[20] takes it to mean that the money-lender used to write ten times the amount. From a statement in Medhatithi[21] on M VIII 41 it appears that money-lenders too coalesced in guild and like guild of traders would reach an understanding with the king by paying him a lump and operating in a manner not permissible under law to achieve maximum gain which was not compatible with sreni dharma. Thus one of the chief causes of poverty was indebtedness and usurious exaction in various ways. Distress was increased by their harassment. By the peculiar love-hate complex people preferred to borrow from private money-lenders, for state loans whatever

15. *On Manu*, VIII, 152.
16. *Ibid*. 169.
17. *Ibid*.
18. *Ibid*.
19. *Op. cit*., p. 165.
20. *Ibid*.
21. P. Niyogi, *Ec. His*., p. 290.

available in the midst of weak economy and turmoil needed urgent repayment.

Endowments

One most effective way out of the usurer's exaction was the distribution of capital from the temples and monasteries through the assemblies and guilds, this capital coming to temple etc. as endowments. Indian epigraphy is replete with such endowments. Some of them have been enlisted in accompanying tables for case study reference to which along with some others will be made in the following sections as a commentary.

The practice of endowment was not merely an act of piety but served a positive economic purpose. The sanctity[22] of a temple property ensured the safe keeping of an endowment and the stability of an investment made through temple. This encouraged donors to deposit funds etc. in temple. Pushpa Niyogi guesses that this might have induced private individuals to deposit money in temple for safe custody only as in a bank according to terms and conditions settled and with no meritorious purpose. Donations of land, livestock, grain, cash or gold were fortwith invested with village assemby or guild or with guilds through villages or town assembly. In many cases, the guilds of oil millers or cattle-rearers or garlanders supplied the offering materials directly as interest in kind on sums received. Otherwise, the assembly measured out interest paddy with which offering materials were procured from the manufacturers of those articles by the assembly or jointly[23] by the assembly and the temple. The endowment used to be permanent, the capital remaining intact and interest accruing perpetually in contravention of the Sastric rule about maximum interest or time limit. The temple also was concerned with the services rendered by the borrowers and returning of the money or things lent.[24] The temple was thus a

22. 1.9 of Ambasamudram Ins. E.I. IX 84f.
23. Spencer, I E S. H R. 1968, p. 292.
24. *Ibid.*

medium for distribution of the economic resources of the society by an inter-penetration of the politico-military, religious and economic spheres.[25] Cattle and gold won by raids into enemy territories were thus channelled into the countryside through village organisations, tying the recipients to the temple services. The linkup of the court and the countryside has been described by Spencer as a politico-economic symbiosis.[26]

The cattle were distributed to the guilds of shepherds[27] who were to provide generally ghee for temple; some of the gold endowed went to some other guild, while donated lands might be earmarked by assembly for persons cultivating for temple services only. Some of these lands came from merchant creditors, who either purchased with money gained in trade in distant towns or acquired them as unredeemed gage. Hence the return of land to agricultural community from merchants or bankers may be noticed as a significant dimension of the temple-merchant symbiosis. Another dimension of the same was the linkup of the urban and rural economy through temple-banking; the donation by a villager might go to town merchants through temple. However, instances of the last type are rare. As an effect of this temple-merchant linkup, the merchants were tied to village. They lost mobility which was vital for advancing business interests and got stuck up with temple management through donations,[28] and sometimes with management villages when villages were assigned to temples as by Bhojasakti.[29] It is not merely for acquiring merit or with the hope of lineage to be fabricated by priests as a scholar[30] speculates but with economic and personal motives partly that they made donations and got in touch with temple management.

One may be permitted to surmise that in making donations the merchants had an eye to their being exempted from

25. Spencer, *Op. cit*, D.C. 1970, p. 434.
26. A Coomaraswamy, Ind. Craftsman, p. 17.
27. Puri, B.N. *History of Gurjara Pratihara*, p. 137.
28. *C.I.I.* IV p. 147 f; R.S. Sharma, Feud. 70-1.
29. D N. Jha in S.C. Sircar Fel. Vol. pp. 119-20.
30. Trade Charters, C.I.I. IV no. 31.

certain religious titles and imposts such as 'Dharma',[31] or to getting advances like housing loans in Kaman and Ahar Inscs.[32] or to ensuring their purchase of the village produces where producers were supplied with necessary capital by the temple, or to securing a market for their goods among the borrowers from the temple; or even they might want to enlist themselves as prospective buyers of grains or goods belonging to the temple openly or clandestinely disposed of by the priests or to a lesser degree as suppliers of the necessities of the temples (other than those provided for by endowments and supplied by villagers at large). Besides, their touch with temple management might give them an easy contact with devadasis.[33]

Endowment of caves or houses engendered a kind of mobility among craftsmen. The architect especially moved with the donor and was exposed to new ideas.[34] Guilds of weavers, metal workers or oil millers were less mobile as they formed a part of the village economy.

Perpetual endowments, especially land, tied monks to monasteries as a scholar[35] rightly points out. They refrained from their duty of wandering and stayed in during and after rainy season, especialy in sowing and harvesting periods. As noted by Itsing rates of rent for monastic lands were exceptionally low. Lands endowed to temples were usually made tax-free by the assembly. Hence there might be a trend to donate land to religious establishments, to take the advantage of low rent and tax exemption, keeping the right to cultivate by some indirect means. This might entail a fall in revenue of the state. Donations brought a change in land ownership from individual to institutional, although this meant no fundamental change in the production pattern. Cultivation was still by individuals, the replacement of its supervision by a village assembly with

31. Kaman—E.I. XXIV 329; Ahar ib., XIX 52.
32. For Bhandarkar's remarks about building of caves as pleasure retreats by merchants in contact with devadasis, see E.I. XXII. p. 31.
33. Vidya Dehejia, *Early Bud. Rock Temples*, p. 146.
34. *Ibid.*, pp. 139-41.
35. *J.B.B.R A.S.* X. 208, 257.

that by a religious establishment was of some significance. The consent of village assembly was necessary all the same for such transfer.[36] Land relations were further affected by change of tenants[37] by donees on donated lands. Doc. VI of Kaman inscription that a donated land was priorly tilled by Brahmana Suhulla, Jajja and others and at the time of gift by Eduvaka. This change of cultivators might have been affected by the gift or slightly prior to the transfer. The same record adds that whatever would be produced was to be added to the capital as was the law of endowment. Dedication of field was not always within the purview of credit unless it was entrusted to some body or its produce was lent out as capital.

Revenue of village donated to meet temple needs[38] similarly had little to do with credit unless it was invested in loaning. When land was entrusted to assembly[39] and the produce to go to charity or worship regularly, it came within credit. The whole or a part of an estate might be distributed on suitable terms by a temple or a monastery to artisans and manufacturers of certain articles to be supplied. Sometimes land was given as site for settling artisans in returns for regular delivery of a part of their outturn according to specified terms. In a Bana insc. from Gudimallam,[40] land purchased from the committee by one of its members was allocated for settling all the oil mills (sekku) of the village thereon as per order of the assembly evidently desired to localisation of the said Industry. The grant[41] by a guild of weavers at Purigere in the form of a proportionate quantity of outturn of the time of R.K. Govinda III does not fall within credit, unless they had received any land or sum from the temple (donee). An oil mill was granted[42] by a Rajanaka chief to god for lamp. The Gwalior Ins. (no. 2) records four donations[43] made by the

36. C. Minakshi, Ad. Soc. Life under the Pallavas, p. 147.
37. Sirpur Ins., E.I. V 38, p. 59.
38. *S.I.I.* III no. 16.
39. E.I. XI 222 f.
40. E I. VI 166.
41. E.I. I, 97.
42. E.I. I, 154.
43. E.I. XXIV, p. 329 f.

inhabitants of the town, a piece of land, two fields, a monthly supply of lamp oil to be made by oilmen's guild @ one palika per mill and a daily supply of fifty garlands of available flowers to be made by a guild of garlands. The piece of land in village Chda Pallika donated to the temple of Navadurga was for a flower garden. If one connects this donation with the supply of flowers by the gardener's guild, the piece of land might have been entrusted to them and the two grain fields donated to temple of Visnu and Navadurga might similarly have been entrusted to the two guilds of oilmen of Sarvesvarapura and Vatsasvamipura. In that case, the endowments would not strictly be separate and four in number, Visnu having his share of garlands though no separate flower garden was allotted, just as the god was to receive in Kamyaka 34 out of 60 garlands to be supplied by a guild of garlanders for one money advance,[44] the rest going to goddess Chamundi. If the fields were allotted to the oil guilds, these were not for setting their mills as they lay in the chief grain-land in village Jayapuraka away from the dwelling places of the guildmen. It may then be presumed that for some reason or other the oilmen were interested in having fields of their own either for the cultivation of oil seeds or for supplementary income which suggests an extra pressure of artisan class on land.

Some other instances of garden endowment are the eleven flower gardens by Pandya Varaguna II Maranjadaiyan[45] in Koluvur along with money for lamp, a flower garden bought with gold[46] from assembly by Manasarpa in the reign of Pallava Kampavarman; a wet land endowed for repair now assigned as flower garden in the 25th year of Aditya Chola[47] and a garden along with village in Nolamba Ayyapa's reign to a Jain Vasti.[48] The income from flower gardens was assigned by merchants to temple for repair (S.I.I. III no. 91). One

44. 137 of 1908.
45. 207 of 1911.
46. 705 of 1909.
47. *B.E I.* X. 54.
48. 666 of 1922.

Kandan, a member of nagarattar, gifted a pasture land in 65th yr. of Nandivarman.[49] In Anjaneri Pls of Bhogasakti,[50] an official Tajavarman adds a colophon to grant a pasture to the merchant corporation (nagara) and fixed 100 rupakas as its price or compensation (niskraya) to the god for which the corporation was to pay the price of guggula annually and in perpetuity to the god as the interest. A village in Goparastra was granted for guggulapuja by the preceptor of Chalukya Pulakesin II.[51]

In an overwhelming majority of cases of endowment in land, gold or cattle, the purpose was the burning of perpetual lamps, of ghee oil or camphor, as the case might be, and of different sizes involving greater or smaller endowment. S.I.I. III no. 53 specifies land for nanda lamp[52] for the worship of Narayana. A later record of Kulottunga[53] throws light on the meaning of lamp burning. Accidental killing of man was punished with death but an order to supply 32 or 48 or 108 cows towards perpetual lamp. It was thus both a punitive and expiatory measure. The cost of cattle or gold would be a fine; it would render a financial assistance to the temple; it was also considered highly efficacious to the merit and prosperity of the donor.

Land for Lamp

Donation of land for lamps is received in S.I.I. I no. 53, III nos. 45, 48, XII no. 58, XIII nos. 306, 324, 325 etc. Land donated for other offerings besides lamp occurs in S.I.I. XII nos. 44, 47, 58, 93 etc. Donations of gold for lamp far outnumber those of cattle or cash, though endowment for lamp of ghee was the most fitting. This was possible because the assembly demanded gold for taking the responsibility to act as guardian of the lamp and other services. While gold endowment mostly came from rich persons, officials and members of royal family, endowments by commoners were in land or cattle, which was

49. *C.I.I.* IV no. 32.
50. I A. IX 123.
51. *Ibid.*
52. *Q J M.S.* Vol. 42 no. 3, p. 99.
53. 696 of 1909. Ins. of Aditya I referring to the gift.

perfectly compatible with limited cash penetration. For instance, 30 cows in 522 of 1905, 96 sheep in 285 of 1911, 100 sheep in 286 of 1911, 180 sheep in 487 of 1904 and some sheep in 188 of 1931, 100 sheep in 142 of 1928 and 90 sheep in 163 of 1931 are all endowments by private individuals. Shepherds donated 96 sheep for lamp in 8 of 1934-5. Cash for lamps was rare; 60 palam Kusu by Varaguna[54] II and 60 Kasu by Nandipotta were both royal grants. An avari (enclosure) for lamp was rare still and along with other purposes.[55] Camphor lamp was rare, for camphor was costly as an import item.[56] A queen provided land for camphor lamp in S.I.I. III no. 48; a chief in Solanadu provided gold for camphor among other things including panchaga vya and sandal in S.I.I. XII no. 92,.by king Varaguna II in no. XV of Tiruchchendur Ins.[57]; also sudha, which generally means mortar, plaster, whitewash or repair etc. may even mean camphor in 1.23 or Kaman Ins.[58] In provisions made for offerings, repair was mentioned in a conventional style in the Volabhi records,[59] while renovation was sometimes the sole purposc as of the prakara and gopura of a Jain temple in 222 of 1911. Sometimes, offerings are detailed as in Tiruchchendur Ins. and Madras Mus. Pls, offerings, services, repairs, festivals and feeding mostly appear with one another among the provisions. In a few cases, provision is specifically made for any of the above, e.g. for festival (Anjaneri charter of Bhogasakti, 209 of 1926 in the 9th yr. of Aditya Chola or 122 of 1928-9 in the end yr. of Nrpatunga), for maintaining servants in temple (155 of 1928), gold for water for bathing or worship (114 of 1914, 227 of 1912). Interesting are donations of cash comfort of the resident monks, especially for clothes,[60] books[61] and academic pursuits[62]

54. Ahar S. Ins.—E.I. XIX, p. 52 f.
55. Camphor Lamp also in S.I.I. III no. 151, S.I.I II-ii p. 126.
56. Cf. Apte. Skt. Eng. Dic.
57. I.A. IX 237.
58. Nalanda S. Ins.; Kanheri nos. 15, 43A, 43B, Mad. Mus. Pls.—pudavaimudal=cloth money.
59. One dramma in Kanheri no. 43B.
60. *S.I.I.* II 574.
61. Kailan C P. of Rata Sridharana—*I.H.Q.* V 23, p. 221.
62. Nalanda C.P. of Devapala—E.I. XVII 310.

e.g. villages to a vidyasthana by Nrpatunga, land for reading and writing Buddhist texts[63] and village for copying manuscripts.[64] Comfort extended to beds, seats and medicines.[65] Specific donations for feeding Brahmanas,[66] ascetics,[67] pilgrims[68] and boys[69] are seen. For regular feeding satra, also known as sadasatra or perpetual feeding house, was maintained.

An important purpose of agrarian economy was served by providing for village tank, separate lands allotted for its upkeep was known as eripatti[70] or erichcheruvu in the south. According to Venkayya the editor of the Gudimallam Ins., a land was set apart out of the produce of which the tank was to be desilted by digging pits in tank Velleri and depositing silt on bund. V. Rangacharya's[71] view that the land was given for digging pits in it and depositing the silt on a local bund does not seem to be correct. In Kampavarman's reign[72] assembly received gold from individuals for the construction or maintenance of a tank on condition of payment by villagers of one kadi of paddy as tank duty on every pattil of land or per crop to the donors. The tank duty is thus transformed into interest in kind for the money received. A (grain?) merchant, Nagan advanced 6400 kadi of paddy to the gana for annual desilt of the village tank as its interest in the 37th yr. of Nandiv II possibly, this merchant of Mamallapuram had lands of his own in the village Payinur. Another grain advance of 1000 kadi from Sadaiyan was received by villagers who pledged themselves to supply 500 kadi of paddy per year

63. Narayana Pala's gr., I.A. XV 309; the editor reads sankha=conch; B C. Sen, Intro. p. XXII. Some Hist. Aspects etc., accept sayana which fits the association.
64. Grains—S.I.I. III no. 8; gold—ib. no. 1; land—237 of 1915.
65. Nalanda S. Ins. E.I. XX 37 f.
66. Gold—263 of 1916.
67. Gold by queen—S.I.I. III no. 94.
68. 285 of 1919, 86 of 1908.
69. Bana Ins. B. from Gudimallam, E.I. XXI 225.
70. V.R.I. p. 479 no. 60.
71. 116 and 402 of 1923.
72. 105 of 1914, V.R. III p. 1598 no. 732.

as well as to close (the sluice of) the tank to collect water for irrigation. Probably, the closing of the tank benefited both the parties with regard to lands lying near it, especially the recipients, whence this high rate of interest. Otherwise, it might simply mean closing of a breach in the bund. In a record[73] of Chola Rajakesari datable to the period from 868 to 898 A.D. Sembiyan made an advance for digging tank retaining a right to levy in crop. There are instances of assembly borrowing from individuals.

Land donated as house-site[74] as well as Vithi[75] or shop and avari or enclosure came much into vogue in this period. Cash endowment to temple either lay idle, unsafe, defalcated or ill-invested, regular payment of interest being affected by disturbed conditions. Hence this trend of investing temple fund in buying and renting house-sites (Doc, IV Ahar Ins.) or houses, shops etc. Even in this safer investment, payment of rent was not regular so that religious obligation was attached. In Doc. VII—Kaman Ins. a conchshell-worker (Sankhika) Bhadra donated two avaris. In Doc. IV—Ahar Ins. four persons gave as surety for the monthly payment of 10 vimsopakas to Kanakasridevi a house-site which had been acquired by their grandfather for a term of 99 years and on which they had constructed inner apartments (apavarakas). The donors (?) enjoin their descendants to enjoy the rent of the house after they had paid the above rent (10 vimsopakas) assigned to the temple. Such endowments do not appear to be free gift out of piety as believed by the editor. The land in question or the purchase money (the lease for 99 years was a conventional clause in the document) was possibly acquired from the temple, with the interest to be paid out of the rent of houses built therein. It is even possible that the sum was originally borrowed from the temple treasury, for some sort the merchant was obliged to assign the rent of a house built therein or a part of the rent to the temple, declaring that the

73. The practice may be traced in the earlier period—Damodarpur C.P. of Budhagupta, Sircar, S.I. 329-30; E.I. XV. 138.
74. Vide, D C. Sircar, *Ep. Gloss.* S.V.
75. The editor of the insc. represents the merchants as "donors".

capital had been spent in buying the house-site and as henceforth the temple would enjoy the rent of the site the question of returning the capital did not arise, nor would the temple be entitled to the whole rent of the house or attach the site as the house was built at their own cost as claimed. In such case, the donors[76] were in fact borrowers (if evasive) and the temple creditor extending housing loans, so to speak. The temple advance is not specified, nor the price of the land; no advance is acknowledged in Doc. VII—Kaman, where Bhadra, the conchshell-worker donated two avaris. Even where the advance has been acknowledged as belonging to goddess Kanakasri (Docs. V, VI, VII—Ahar), the sum is not specified nor the purchase money of the avaris. From the silence it may be suspected that a part of the purchase advance above the price was misappropriated. It is also possible, though less likely in the light of the manner in which the transactions are reported in the above cases that the temple itself bought the houses and rented them indirectly through persons who took the responsibility to discharge the temple's share. This was very near subletting on a lease basis. As such experimentations were not paying, the gosthi itself purchased with temple money a portion of building site with a dwelling for utilisation by the temple as in Doc. V—Ahar. Also in Doc. VIII—Kaman, the gosthikas or managing committees of the temple themselves bought two avarikas containing south facing vithis in cattle market (Kambuli hatta=ox-fair from dewlap of a bull), let them out to realise the expenses of whitewash (or camphor ?), vermilion, lights etc. with the drammas formerly made over by Bhogadeva. According to the editor Mirashi, Bhoja made over this amount to Pramanarasi who gave it to Chamundaka, and after his death the acharya Chamundaka, it is supposed, paid the amount to the gosthikas who now purchased the avarikas with those drammas.

We prefer to interpret Pramanarasi and Chamundaka not as names of priests; Chamundaka[77] denoted the acharya of the temple of Chamunda with whom Bhoja originally deposited the

76. Cf. Bana C.P.—E.I. XIX no. 2.
77. I. 22-23.

sum to be used as a loan capital.[78] In mathematical literature Pramanarasi denotes the first term in a rule of three i.e. the principal or capital in an interest sum.[79] Such terms crept into epigraphic documents of perpetual capital possibly as a result of the spread of commercial education,[80] comprising exchange, accounts and interest work that characterised this age. The fourth case-ending in Pramanarasi may be explained by a Panian rule to mean placed to be used as principal.[81] But as there was no demand for, or little gain and much risk, in loaning, the sum lay idle, and when the acharya was no more, some other acharya whose name might have occurred in the last portion, and members of the managing committee invested the money in the safe novel way. The other six purchases in Kaman were affected by Sauvarnika mahajana with temple fund from merchants or Brahmanas showing collusion between the merchant community and the temple management and the seventh by the temple committee, whereas in Kaman one purchase was by a conchshell-worker besides that by the committee. Doc. VIII—Ahar shows control exercised by Sauvarnika mahajana in the management of the temple fund and payment of it. It also indicates that Sarvasa's agreement to pay 10 Vimsopakas monthly out of the rent of a house probably failed or was not considered sufficient; hence fresh deed making over the entire rent, presumably exceeding 10 vimsop, was done with two Ksatriyas and two ladies. It seems that the new rent contractors including the women had an eye to making extra income from the apartments by some questionable means.

In a Bhilsa inscription of 878 A.D.,[82] a merchant Hatia bought three vithis from persons, at least one of whom was a merchant to assign their rent as aksayani (vi) ka to the temple-complex of Bhailaswami. The rent of the first, pa

78. Cf Apte, Dic. II.
79. Cf. Pirenne, Ec. Soc. His. of Med. Europe, p. 124.
80. Chaturthi by Panini II 3. 14-15.
81. E.I. XXX. 2. 11 f; Sircar, *Stud. Rel. Life*, p. 119 f.
82. A heavy copper coin, according to Sircar, like Yaudheya dramma, cf. Smith, Cat. of coins in Ind. Mus., p. 182, coin no. 18b.

(panchiyakadramma)[83] 13 or 130, was endowed to Narayana; the rent of the second, pa 50, and of the third, pa 40, were made over to Mothers to meet the expenses of niyata bhoga (regular offerings). Dr. Sircar thinks that the donor intended that the vithis themselves could be utilised (samalabhya). The Baijnath Prasasti (778-878 A.D.), a Rajanaka chief of kiragrama donates a punyasala to temple.[84]

Gold Endowment

Cases of gold endowments were numerous. Any offer of gold, from an insignificant[85] 3 and 5 Kalanju[86] to 736 or 570 Kal.[87] was solicited by the village assemblies. Sometimes the assembly received gold from the temple directly. In 22nd yr. of Chola Vijayalaya (Parakesari—9th cent.) two assemblies received 250 Kal. of gold from temple[88] and agreed to measure out interest paddy to provide for certain offerings and another 50 Kal. for a higher interest. Similarly, in Kampavarman's reign (9th cent.) assembly received 24 Kal. It is possible that in such cases the assembly marked out certain lands from the produce of which they measured out the interest paddy, without formally transferring the said land wholly to the temple. In the cases of land endowments the transfer was formally made by assembly by an exemption of the taxes after receiving land price in gold directly from the donor and indirectly from the temple. The convention of making land tax-free for temple was mostly followed.[89] In fact, in such cases, the interest on the whole amount comprised the exempted taxes as well as the price of the materials to be supplied regularly so it may be argued that materials to be supplied stood for the interest of a major portion of the gold, the rest accounting for the

83. E.I. I p. 97, 1.30.
84. 18 of 1920.
85. 162 of 1912, 406 N 1905. S.I.I. III no. 94.
86. 391 of 1905—lady to assembly in Kampa's reign.
87. Pandya Varaguna donated this high amount to nagarattar for specified offerings—360 of 1921.
88. Mad. Mus. Pls.—S.I.I. III no. 128.
89. 202, 209 of 1907; 435 of 1905—by Nambi Appi in 18th yr. of Aparajita.

exempted taxes. The assembly received gold for land[90] in no. 45, S.I.I. II from a native of Kanchipuram. To 100 rupakas in Bhogasakti's charter may have been the price of the pasture and not a separate endowment. That the assembly was in great need of gold or cahs is thus strongly indicated. It sold the right of collecting the market fees of the bazar street for 25 kasu in Nalur to the temple in the 2nd year of Aditya.[91] In such cases, the taxes represented the interest on the money received as perpetual capital. The sabha and ur of village spent up an endowment gold for the specified purpose of lamp upon constructing a bathing mantapa and had to provide for the said lamp from a land.[92] The assembly of Kalutur also made over 1/3 of the income from a local lake to temple. The assembly sold the right of collecting 1 kadi of paddy per crop for the upkeep of a tank to a person in Kampavarman's reign.[93] Taken with the former sale of taxes and income from lake this assignment of grain levy does not seem to be an act of piety or charity, except if that person made over the levy to a temple.

Taxes and Dues Assignment

Assignment of taxes and dues as acts of charity are seen in other records. Nagavardhana, the preceptor of Pulakesin II, assigns dues and taxes and the revenue of 8 villages to temple.[94] Tax collected by perunagarattar was assigned by merchant community to a Jain matha in the 2nd year of Aditya I. Bhogasakti arranged for holding the annual Yatra festival of a deity for a fortnight from the octroi and other dues from merchants—1 rupaka on each cart ingress and egress at Jayapura, 100 rupakas in E. Trikuta, 200 rupakas in W. Mahagirihara, 100 rupakas in E. Mahagirihara and 50

90. Hultzsch's assumption that 40 kal. of gold was the price of the land (2 nilam 1900 kuli) seems to be correct, as the purpose of offerings mentioned for gold and land are the same.
91. *S.I.I.* III no. 90.
92. 349 of 1911.
93. 402 of 1923.
94. I.A. IX 123, 237. C.I.I. IV p. 147, l. 35-39; *JBBRAS* XX p. 1-10. 17.

rupakas in palludhamba, in all 450 krsnaraja rupakas (excluding perhaps the octroi at Jayapura which could not remain fixed). The merchants, exempted from the taxes were to celebrate the festival. One rupaka per day by Maitraka Dhruvasena II to be perpetually paid to temple was evidently a kind of cess called dharmadaya. A Rajanaka chief allotted 6 drammas daily out of the collection at mandapika (custom house).[95] Assignment of self-imposed taxes for having taken money advances were not acts of generosity. A potter's guild living in Kamyaka[96] in consideration of a sum received in advance stipulated to pay a permanent cess—one para per wheel every month. A guild of masons agreed to pay one dramma per member per month for a similar advance. Unlike the guild of glorists these two guilds paid in cash, as the articles they manufactured were not among the regular requirements of the temple. The editor notes that the guild sometimes paid out of its common fund[97] but believed a cess on its members as the money advances must have been spent on purposes useful to all members. The editor also refers to a provision in Br. (XVIII-11, 13) for the guild to impose a fine on defaulting members. In fact, the cess was the interest on the capital advance never to be paid back. But the interest here could not be static, nor the rate of interests as a whole could be ascertained. The temple would be deprived of its due return in case the guild broke up or changed place or if there was a fall in membership.

Probably, this possibility created the necessity of buying and renting avari and vithi which too was not free from risk as seen.[98] In another case of self-imposed taxes assigned to temple we are not told whether this was in view of some money advance. Rather the term dharma applied to this tithe reminds one of dharmadaya of the Valabhi record and reveals its nature in attaining religious merit. Certain horse-dealers who met at the horse fair[99] at Pehoa agreed to impose upon

95. E.I. p. 97, Baijnath Pr. 1.27.
96. Kaman, 1. 16-17.
97. Doc—V, Kaman L. 19.
98. P. Niyogi, *Op. cit.*, p. 255.
99. Cf. Pirenne, *Op. cit.*, pp. 8-9, 14f.

themselves and their customers certain taxes or tithes which were to be distributed among some temples, priests and sanctuaries. They were 33-34 in number and belonged to several countries. Two dharmas were to be deducted from the sum received by a dealer for each animal sold. One dharma was to be paid by the buyer in addition to the price (the king or any other buyer in Prthudaka and only the king in Traighataka and other sacred places). The editor takes a dharma not as the name of a coin but a religious impost to be settled by custom. The money thus collected was given as aksayanivi. According to the editor, it did not mean that the money was to be invested and its interest alone was to be spent, for the document contains no clause referring to an investment; but the term aksayanivi contains that implication. It gives rules for the distribution of the shares and it clearly indicates that the tax is to be levied not once but perpetually on all sales. The amount of the case therefore depending on sales could not remain constant. The donees were : (1) a temple at Kanauj, (2) another temple at Kanauj, (3) Visnu temple near Kanauj, (4) Visnu temple at Pehoa, (5) the Pujakal and (6) the sthana (sanctuary). The shares were 7/24 of the tax paid by merchants for the first donee, each a like amount of the same for the second and the third, 1/24 of the same and 6/12 of the tax from customers for the fourth, 1/24 of the tax from merchants and 2/12 from customers for the fifth and 1/24 of the former and 4/12 of the latter of the last. Gosthikas or the management (of the temple) were to collect the money.[100]

It is possible that dharma,[101] if not a mistake for dramma as suggested by some, was a percentage that amounted to a dramma as normally such a tithe on every animal was found to be in slightly later times. Niyogi finds here an instance of private individuals introducing a tax binding on all persons including the king.[102] It is strange that a group of horse dealers were entitled to bind their buyers including the king in

100. E.I. I 184 f.
101. Kosambi takes it to be a religious impost with a query, *J.E.S.H.O.* v. 2, p. 281.
102. Ibid., p. 198.

the matter of assigning a cess to religious bodies unless that was a customary rate. Besides, most of them were probably foreigners as they belonged to different countries, horse being an import commodity; as such they are not expected to make the grant out of devotion. Practically, the tax was imposed and realised periodically, when the traders arrived, and ceased when the fair was over. The inclusion of the king was to give a stamp of compulsion to the rate, which might have had some adverse effect on horse-trade. It appears from analysis that a horse-dealer and a buyer (where not exempted) each paid one dharma (a percentage) per animal. The buyer paid that to the seller in excess of the actual price and the temple committee collected two such from the dealer. One paid by the latter himself and the other paid to him by the buyer during sale. for it would be impracticable for the person appointed by the temple committee to collect the impost from the buyer at the time of each sale; hence two dharmas were to be deducted from merchants, which is also suggested by the inscriptional passage.[103] General buyers were exempted from paying dharma at places except Pehoa. The king is not said to have been exempted, perhaps because he was the chief buyer, but it may not be out of place to guess that he was exempted at Kanauj. For the Kanauj temples were not entitled to shares of buyer's tithes as well, while the Pehoa temple was allotted shares of the collections from both the dealer and the buyer. Of course, the distribution was not area-wise and the tithes if paid at all by king Kanauj would be shared by temples at Pehoa just as the Kanauj temple would have its share of tithes paid by dealers at places other than Kanauj.

Assignment of taxes,[104] e.g. on ghee, to village 'mahajanas' (assembly men) to be used for communal purposes does not fall within credit, unless it is assumed that the king had received an amount from the assembly. Like dedication of caves (e.g. layana by Malada in Nalanda—St. Ins.) or halls, donations of money not recorded as perpetual capital fetching

103. Ibid.
104. Nilgund Ins. E.I. VI 101-2; Didpur Ins. 253; Soratur Ins. of 866 A.D., I.A. XII, 258.

interest are outside of credit, unless it is assumed to have been invested in loaning.

Cash Endowment

Cash endowments are fewer in number in consonance with the limited cash nexus. The greatest donor of cash and gold of the period was Pandya Varaguna II. He entrusted 1400 Kasu to a temple with the express stipulation that the money should be lent out to meet certain expenses with its interest. the capital remaining in fact (L. 4-5, Tiruchchendur Ins.).[105] The money was divided into 16 unequal parts and invested with different bodies @ 2 kalam of paddy per Kasu per yr. In L-3-4 of his Ambasamudram Ins. recording the gift of another sum (290 kasu) interest is said to have been taken in such a way that the cash is not destroyed.[106] An ins. of Aditya I (969 of 1909) refers to a previous gift of 60 palamkasu made by the same Pandya king. One of his predecessors Sodaiya Maran donated 100 kasu for lamp. In his reign a Brahmin lady donated 10 dinaras. In Kanheri,[107] a Buddhist from Gauda country made an endowment of 100 drammas, and one Visnu 100, 40, 40, and 120 dras (300 dras in total). Nandivarman III donated 60 kasu (a later copy of some original record ?).[108] In Kaman Ins., Bhojadeva donated a sum of drammas.

Grain Endowment

Endowments of grain are recorded in several places. In Kampavarman's reign one Sadaiyan made over 1000 kadi of paddy to villagers of Utkar for closing the tank for irrigation.[109] He gave another 400 kadi to feed Brahmanas.[110] Perhaps the largest grain endowment was from Nagan, a merchant of Mamallapuram, received by the gana of Payinur in 37th yr. of VII for desilting the village tank.[111] Grant of 100

105. *E.I.* XXI. 10(.
106. *E.I.* IX 84.
107. *A.I.* XIII 123.
108 120 of 1928-9 (S I.I XII no. 60).
109 *S.I.I.* III no. 5.
110. Ibid., no. 8.
111. 109 of 1932-3 (S.I.I XII no. 34).

kadi of paddy by a lady is recorded in Aditya's reign.[112] A Brahmin lady donated 40 kadi of paddy in 15th yr. of Nrpatunga.[113] Bana Chandiyanna remitted the income from the levy called ponnatere to the mahajanas in lieu of 120 ganduga of paddy on the occasion of solar eclipse. Evidently, the king did not receive the grain and it was deposited with the temple. Against this the remission of levy would be an act of piety. Hence this was an instance of endowment of grain which was in fact borrowed from the assembly, the remitted levy constituting the interest.

Donors

A wide variety is seen in the composition of donors from kings, princes,[114] officials[115] and merchants[116] to priests[117] and pilgrims,[118] from artisans like goldsmith[119] and conchshell worker[120] to shepherds[121] and horse-dealers[122] and from queens[123] and Brahmin ladies[124] to mistresses and temple prostitutes. The temples recorded the gifts of the concubines of kings and chieftains side by side with those of their queens. That some of them were songstresses and dancing girls is indicated by lavish gifts they obtained from royal personages.[125]

In the 11th yr. of Aditya I, his mistress (bogiyar= bhogastri) Nangai Satta Parumanan granted 30 Kal. for lamp to Mahadeva.[126] In this 14th yr. she donated another 30 Kal.

112. 168 of 1904.
113. 258 of 1912.
114. Anjaneri, *C.I.I.* VI 147.
115. 113, 114 of *S.I.I.* XII, Chera Ins. B. *E.I.* V. 38. p. 37.
116. 283 of 1919; *S.I.I.* XVI no. 53.
117. 48 of 1914—no. 58 of *S.I.I.* XII; *I.A.* IX 123, 435 of 1905.
118. Kanheri, *I.A.* XIII no. 42.
119. *S.I.I.* III no. 42.
120. D VII—Kaman—*E.I.* XXIV. 329.
121. 8 of 1934-5—*S.I.I.* XII no. 54.
122. *E.I.* I 184 (Pehoa).
123. *S.I.I.* III nos. 46-48, 300 of 1901, etc.
124. 258 of 1912, 135 of 1908.
125. *A.R.E.* (Madras, Sept. 1918), p. 13—no. 14.
126. 105 of 1931 (*S.I.I.* XIII no. 219).

for lamp which the assembly of the village spent up in constructing a mantapa.[127] In the 4th yr. of Aparajita Amatti, the mistress of a chief Vayirameghavarman, donated 30 kal. for lamp in the temple of Tirruvorriyur[128] (equal to the amount donated by the queen of Aparajita in the 7th yr.)[129] The same year Patradini, another mistress of the same chief, donated an equal sum.[130] Each sum was invested with the sabha and amrtagana of Adambakkam. An old Cannarese insc. of W. Chalukya Vijayalaya records the gifts of one of his concubines, the harlot Vinapoti, a ruby pedestal, silver umbrella and a field for the support of the idol. She was pranavallabha or heart's darling to the king and daughter of Kuchipoti and grand-daughter of Revamanchal. The field was called mangalulle of 800 measures.[131] Another insc.[132] records grants made by one of the harlots of the temple of Virupaksa in the reign of Dhruva Dharavarsa; Badipoddi, the daughter of Govindapoddi, a harlot of the temple of the queen Kijanahadevu had previously made certain costly gifts and now gave a land and ubhayamukhi.[133] In the 4th yr. of Aditya I, Sendan Sayyavaymani, a servant (dancing girl) of the Tiruvarangam temple donated 10 kal. to the temple Mahadeva at Srikanta Chaturvedimangalam for burning twilight and supply of bathing water.[134] The upasakas of the temple accepted the gift and responsibility.

Joint Endowment

Donations made jointly by temple committee,[135] religious community,[136] town organisation,[137] merchant corporation[138]

127. 284 of 1911 (*S.I.I.* XIII no. 247).
128. 158 of 1912 (ib no. 87).
129. 163 of 1912 (ib no. 91).
130. 161 of 1912 (ib no. 88).
131. *I.A.* XI 105.
132. *I A.* XI 125.
133. Ibid.
134. 114 of 1914 (S.I.I. XII no. 88).
135. Ibid.
136. 190 of 1912—Community of Mahesvaras.
137. Gwalior Ins., ib.
138. 222 of 1911.

or village assembly[139] or by their individual members[140] are well on record. Sometimes more than one individual made a single endowment.[141] Sometimes, a donor belonging to a different sect made gift to a religious establishment. Somavamsi king Mahasivagupta (7th cent. first half) who was a worshipper of Siva granted village Kailasapura in Chhattisgarh to community of monks of Buddhist monastery.[142] This was another instance of the rapproachement among common worshippers[143] of different sects noticed in Bengal and elsewhere in this period, before and after. However we do not find a common peasant, fisherman or the like in this milieu of donors; perhaps his means did not match his religious aspiration. Or perhaps no record was kept for paltry amounts donated by them. And we have instances of assembly and guilds receiving gold directly from temple, no names of donors occurring in the record.[144]

Donees

Next to the temples of Siva and Visnu leaving aside sun-god[145] and Mother-goddess[146] the monasteries of the Buddhist[147] and Jains[148] were the chief recipients. Sometimes, priests[149] and monks[150] were named as donees. We have also found land etc.

139. 705 of 1909 (*S.I.I.* XIII no. 314) land by Sabha.

140. 6?6 of 1922 (ib XII no. ?8) a member of nagarattar; nos. 315, 324 of *S I.I.* XIII—a headman; 327 of 1912—a member of ganattar.

141. 256 of 1922—3 Kadi of paddy by 5 persons; 487 of 1904—180 sheep by 2 persons; 91 of 1913.

142. Millar Pls. E.I. V. 23. 114.

143. Sircar, *Studies in Rel. Life*, p. 186; Niyogi, *J.A.I.H.* V. 5. p. 171.

144. Mad. Mus. Pls; ib; E.I. V. 24 329.

145. *E.I.* IX. p. 1f., XIII 121.

146. Doc. VIII—Kaman.

147. *I.A.* XIII 133; *E.I.* VI 287, XXII 66, IX 116, XVII 310, XXIII 114; *I.H.Q.* XXIII 221; *J.A.S.* (Let.) VII no. 2. p. 83; etc.

148. 304 of 1900-1, 348 of 1901, *E.I.* XXI 138 etc.

149. Peheva Ins. (Donee no. 5).

150. *E.I.* XXXVIII p. 59; *M.A.S.B.*, I 85.

to be endowed for the upkeep of tank,[151] Satra,[152] sanctuary[153] and Vidyasthana.[154] As it has been mentioned above, some donations had an academic interest, e.g. in the Pala king's grant to the Nalanda monastery at the request of the Sailendra king. As there was provision for copying manuscripts, it may be guessed that some copies went to Sumatra.

It is interesting to note that the donees themselves mostly do not appear to have invested the money or other endowments with guilds or assemblies, although it is well known that temples and monasteries engaged in lending business.[155] G.L. Adhya[156] questions the proposition of Kosambi that monasteries supplied the working capital to caravaneers, "Had the monasteries themselves been engaged in business, especially when they required liquid money to supply loans as had been suggested why was money invested in the guilds ?" Apart from the fact that temple fund was sometimes invested with assemblies and guilds directly by temples without any reference to donors, or that donors stated the expected interest with no reference to a guild or assembly, investment made through the donor himself was probably necessary for passing on him the onus of lending money at interest which did not befit priests and monks according to norms. Even in clear cases of money advance taken straightway from temple, the cess or commodities to be regularly paid in fact as interest is euphemistically called aksayanivi instead of vrddhi or the like. It was also perhaps necessary to enlist the donor as the most important witness to the transaction as well as to make him bear in full or share the expenses of recording the same. Any way, as recipients of interest the religious establishment would have to manage the transactions themselves, for the donor would soon be out of the picture. Plausibly, the investment with a particular body or person of established credit would be suggested by the

151. 283 of 1919; *E.I.* IX 225 etc.
152. 347 of 1914 etc.
153. Peheva Ins.
154. *S.I.I.* II 574.
155. Kasambi, *Op. cit.*
156. *Early Ind. Econ.*, p. 99.

donees who were in a better position to know who would maintain the regular supply of interest materials.

Guilds had earned much credibility in handling public money and the donors from a king to a commoner was satisfied when his deposit was entrusted to them, so much so that investments were no longer announced in town assembly (nigama sabha) as in earlier period (E.I. VIII no. 122). Altekar[157] observes that like guild-banks[158] village communities also had their own banks of sufficient economic stability. Mahajanas or assembly men in Karnataka received deposits or assignment of taxes to spend on work of public utility. It is also guessed that they had banks under their management or loaned the amounts through private money-lenders under their control. Of this link operation we have hardly any evidence. But as trustees of public money,[159] guilds suffered competition from temple treasury,[160] at once static, stable and sanctified, and partly stood in relation to the latter as subsidiary banks to a central bank. Guilds of the floating type, prone to change places owing to disturbances, could not be considered as fit bodies for investment. In fact, guilds which received advances or investments in the endowment records were tied to a locality by the nature of their work, e.g. guilds of garlanders (Malikasreni), of shepherds (Kottamanradi), oil millers (Kolhukasreni), potters (Kumbhakarasreni or artisans (sthapatis who were settled, excepting those who were a bit mobile). Even certain mercantile communities (nagaratar) were losing mobility for reasons discussed and were getting tied to a temple or a village.

Assemblies

A major share of the endowments in the form of cash, gold, cattle or grain went to village assemblies (Brahminical sabha

157. Ibid., p. 371, 208 f.
158. K.V. Virji, p. 222—guild banks in Valabhi—*E.I.* XI 112. D.R. Das, *Econ. Hist. Deccan*, p. 274.
159. Sabha acted as public treasury—cf. Mahalingam, Banas in *S. Ind. His.*, pp. 287-8.
160. L. Gopal, *Op. cit.*, p. 81.

and non-Brahmanicalur) as investment for redistribution of the resources in the countryside. The assembly in Kalattur has been styled perumakkal. We have also got a reference to urar of Kalattur (283 of 1919). The sabha or some of its committees was called amrtagana[161] in the inscriptions of Aparajita at Tirruvorriyur (in Saidapet taluk, Chingleput dist. in Madras). In 159 of 1912 again gold for lamp etc. was deposited with Karmakkilvar[162] of Tirruvoriyur. The assembly men in the management of endowments were called mahajanas in Karnataka, perumakkal in Tamil country and mahattaras in S. Gujerat and Maharastra.[163] In 435 of 1905 Nambi Appi's grant of land obtained from sabha was entrusted with dharmigal, perhaps a body that looked after endowments. The terms of the endowment in 345 of 1906 were agreed upon by tirunamakkilavar of Ulaichcheri. In the Ambasamudran Ins. and 283 of 1916, members of Variyam (committee) were nominated to see the assembly maintain the charity for the gold it received. In recording a grant it was customary in Karnataka to write that having laved the feet of so many mahajanas the donor made an assignment (e.g. of a tax) for public benefit.[164] It need not be taken literally, for it is too much to believe that a donor chief would wash or even appoint somebody to wash the feet of some hundreds of villagers for the sake of showing high reverence.

However, this esteem was the basis of high credit enjoyed by village assemblies, and there is little scope of belief, as C. Minakshi[165] states and D.N. Jha[166] suggests, that the merchant community was preferred to village assembly for investment. They refer to the inscription of Marambadevi, the queen of Nandi Varman III prob. (303 of 1901), where a devadana was entrusted to cloth-merchants (aruvaivanigar) of Srikanthapuram who according to the former (p. 139), were preferred

161 *E.I.* XI. 224.
162. *J.E.S.H.R.*, Oct. 65, p. 153.
163 Altekar, *The Rastrakutas*, p. 205; *mahattara* means guild-elders in C. Indian records.
164. *I.A.* XII p. 216.
165. *Ad. Soc. Life under Pallavas*, p. 139.
166. S.C. Sircar, Fel. Vol. p. 141 f.

to village assembly for their interest shown. But this was one of the few stray cases where endowment was invested with merchants. In Anjaneri charter, villages and money assigned to temple were to be managed by nagarattar (merchants in groups of 5 to 10 or 15) for holding Yatra or religious procession with commercial fair). A large amount of gold by Pandya Varaguna was invested with nagarattar (360 of 1921 — no. 71 of S.I.I. XII). Of several donations of Pandya king of the same name who may be considered the greatest single donor of cash and gold in this period a cash of 120 kasu was entrusted to a nagarattar and many other sums invested with assemblies. Statistics confirm that a bulk of the endowment money was entrusted to village assemblies in this period and after.

Distribution Pattern

The Tiruchchendur grant of the said king offers an opportunity to analyse the distribution pattern of a good number of investments in one single document.[167] The total sum of 1400 kasu was entrusted in 16 unqual parts to different bodies of sabhai (= assembly in Brahmadeya village), urar (assembly usually found in non-Brahmadeya village) and nagarattar[168] (a commercial guild of a town). Of the 16 transactions, 15 were made with village assemblies and only 1 with town merchants. The total amount going into the hands of villagers was 1280 kasu i.e. 91.43% of the total investment, while the amount received by merchants was 120 kasu 4 urar, while the regionwise distribution was as follows : Kudanadu divn. covering 4 Sabhas and 3 urs had the largest allotment (7 cases out of 16), Valudivalanadu—4, Parantaka valanadu 3, Srivallabha and Amitagana 1 each. While no one village received loan more than once, investments were not evenly distributed. The same was true of Valudi allotments. The breakup shows that of 278 kasu invested in the division, sabhai received 51%, ur 5.9% and nagarattar 43.16%. The sabhai received the major share here as in the general investment pattern (91.43% of the

167. Ibid.
168. Ibid.

total). Also in Kudanadu divn. which had the largest allotments (730 kas, or little more than 52%), the sabha was well ahead of the urar, receiving 440 kas. (60.20%), while ur received 290 kas (less than 40%) only. This high preference in advancing loans to, or the high demand of credit by, the Brahminical assemblies was not depending on the concessional rate of interest prescribed in the sastras; rather this inscription places Brahmanas and non-Brahmanas on a par in charging interest at the same rate at least when they operated in organised bodies and belies the Smrti contention. The question of security also did not perhaps determine unequal distribution, for in that case the rate of interest would have differed. May be, the preference was due to a belief that there was merit in meeting the credit needs of the Brahmanas.

Besides, caste links and kinship bonds among the committee members of the temple and assembly may have inspired this preference. Or probably, the reasons were economic and the credit needs of the Sabhai were greater than those of urs. As to security, it may be argued that organisationally the urs might be weaker than the Sabhai. Again non-Brahminical members of ur were cultivators themselves who could be evicted whenever their lands would be donated or transferred, whereas the connection between individual owners and land appears to have been stronger in a Brahmadeya village.[169] Eviction would shake the economic stability of urar, undermine the security of loans advanced to them and lower their credit. Yet it has to be noted neither credit demand nor security let of an organisation had any repercussion on the rate of interest in this record. Although evidences are scanty to substantiate the explanations or to say that this condition prevailed in many parts of the south (for we find the same king entrusting a high amount 570 kal. to nagarathar), the fact remains that in the said record the assemblies, and of them the sabhai especially, received bulk of the resources invested, and if this examination serves as a typological study, that happened to be the general trend. Bonafides must have been a factor of greater importance

169. Cf. N. Karashima, *J.E.S.H.R.*, Jun. 66, p. 154.

when a loan was advanced to an individual effecting change in the rate of interest. We do not find the terms on which an endowment land was entrusted by the ur[170] or Palkalam to a drummer, who resided in the village and probably belonged to the staff of the temple to be served. This rather meant a shift from the cultivation of the land being conducted by the ur. We notice here two things: (i) a formal change of cultivator by assembly on a donated land or entrusting the land by village assembly secondarily to a resident; (ii) the person did not belong to the agricultural community but earned a living by beating drum (udakkai). It may be surmised that sometimes the donor kept the endowment with himself, agreeing to pay the interest amount regularly. This rests on problematical interpretations. In Kanheri Ins. the donor stated that the perpetual endowment was for his own use so long as he lived.[171] It meant the money and not the hall which was another gift. In any case, he would have to stay in Western India far away from his country Gauda to observe the terms of endowment, keeping it with himself. Rather, as the succeeding lines speak of the refixation of interest after the donor's death, the passage quoted probably intends to say that enjoyment by the monks of the interest was to be according to the terms fixed by the donor so long as he lived, which were to be revised after his demise.

170. *S.I.I.* XII no, 114—152 of 1916.
171. *I.A.* XIII no. 15.

4

Merchant Bankers—Kinds of Loan and Interest—Rates of Interest

(FROM 900-1200 A.D.)

The period from 900 to 1200 A.D. saw a recovery of India's participation in foreign trade. The revival in trade and urbanisation was marked in Gujerat, Rajasthan and South India in the 11th-12th century. The trade with China revived in the 10th century. The Chinese preferred the sea-route to India[1] to the central Asian route in this period probably on account of the political chaos in the north-west of India and the Arab settlements in Sindh. Hemp, sugar and luxury goods brought gold from China.[2] In Tanjore an endowment was made in Chinese gold which confirms the dominance of the Cholas in Far-Eastern trade beating the Arab in competition. Arab traders could assert more in the Western Indian marts,[3]

1. The vessels from China and Sindh (Arab) came to Broach, according to Al Indrisi, Elliot and Dowson, I 121. The presence of the Chinese ships up to Aden noticed by Arab geographers and the lack of knowledge among the Chinese about the sea-route from Quilon to the Persian Gulf may be explained by a surmise that technically equipped Chinese ships used to be hired by the merchants of other notions. The Chinese claim to have first devised the rudder which accounts for increased tonnage ; cf. D.R. Chanana in Reading in *Ind. Econ. Hist.*, ed. B.N. Ganguli, p. 6.
2. China had to pass an order in 1296 to stop the gold drain; R.S. Sharma, *Ind. Feud.*, p. 250f.
3. Prab. Chin, p. 102 ; L. Gopal, *Op. cit.*, p. 132 f.

where they vied with Indian business magnates like Vastupala and Tejabpala and incurred the apathy of the pratiharas and the Gahadavalas for commercial reasons. The rate of profit in sea trade especially in the south must have been high enough to encourage high rates of interest on sea loans. India spent much of this profit on costly imports including horse and had not much bullion left to build up a currency of good standard though it had revived from its previous eclipse.

The revival of gold and other coins might be due to resumption of the supply of gold from Africa that had been interrupted during the Arab invasion, but contact with the central Asian sources of silver supply could not be resumed and silver became scarce.[4] Gadnaiya coins were preponderant in Rajputana, but both gold and silver were debased in the coinages of the Kalachuri, Shahi, Gahadavala, Chandella and Chalukya Kings. The supply of metal from China as known from Vaijayanti (p. 43) could not be a real substitute. The growing use of money, though debased and therefore not prized much by foreign traders who wanted Indian goods against their own, had a significance within the country, and monetary loans secured by pledges in the north and endowments of hard cash in the south were a powerful link in its circulation. The circulation could not reach up to an extent to wipe out interest realised from bodily labour. Money promoted internal trade. Samadeva mentions market place where merchants of other countries came.[5] Small dealers were known as Krayanaka in Damodara of the Gahadavala court[6] who refers to bankers strict in their transactions.[6a]

Merchant Bankers

Although foreign writers like Al Idrisi and Marco Polo praise the fidelity of Indian merchants, there is a mass of evidence to the contrary. It may be that they dealt well with

4. Cf. Thakur, *J E.S.H.O.* XIV, p. 285; gold and silver=1 : 8, despite regional and other variations; Maity, *Op. cit.*, p. 172.
5. *Yasastilaka*, 33. Cf. Anekant (Hindi), vol. 18. no. 2, p. 50f.
6. *Uktivyakti*, p. 39 l.8, p. 45 l.8.
6a. Ib., p. 23.

the foreign traders and fleeced their countrymen. Siddhrsi refers to their profit-mongering without a qualm of conscience.[7] The writer of the Trisasti holds that a man of trading profession who is not a cheat is seldom found.[8] In Prab. Chin. (92), King Siddharaja was unwilling to associate with a merchant in building a temple by taking money from him. Ksemendra and Kalhana refer to the utter dishonesty of merchant bankers. This picture of the Kashmirian society was perhaps true of all parts of the country. The Jain bankers became a dominant group in the social polity in Gujerat, so that Kumarapala had to depend on their support in his rise to power[9] and on their financial assistance when wars depleted his treasury. In the south, Vira-Bananju merchants who invoked Bhagavati and some Jain deities captured commerce in and outside the country, coalesced in large bodies like Chambers of Commerce, e.g. the Nanadesis, Svamis, Setthis etc., had operations abroad and possessed warrior bands.[10]

Organised free booters and anti-social elements were active in parts of the country.[11] Cattle raids and looting of the peasantry continued in full swing.[12] Somadeva and Ksemendra refer to plunder by a petty grantee (Samanta).[13] Depredations caused by Muslim raiders, wars and succession feuds that characterised 11th-12th cent. impeded agriculture and wiped out social security.[14] The capture of agriculturists, householders, traders and bankers is described in the Manasollasa.[15] Floods of the Palar (428 of 1905, 322 of 1906) and the Kaveri (214 of 1911) and famine (397 of 1913) in the south led to alienation of land and to borrowings by the assemblies. Repeated famines in Kashmir shot up the prices and we have

7. Ibid.
8. Ibid.
9. Ray, *Dynastic Hist. of N. India*, pp. 976, 997.
10. K.A.N. Sastri, *Colas*, p. 595.
11. Cf. Moti Chandra, Intro. Ibid., p. 83.
12. E.C. IV Hg 79, etc. Sewell, *Hist. Insc. S.I.*, p. 93.
13. Br. Kathama, III 200 f.
14. Cf B P. Mazumdar, *Socio. Econ. Hist.*, p. 170.
15. I Vs 1043.

evidences of house holders living on borrowed rice.[16] The state showed no concern for relief, encouraged profiteers and imposed fresh imposts. Some kings practised ruthless spoilation of temple property.[17] In such a scene large scale migration of people from one place to another was a natural sequel and hoarding of wealth[18] was a common phenomenon. Nagara (merchant?) Brahmins had migrated to Benaras from the Gujerat in 12th century[19] and investment of money in lending was a remote possibility. The creditor therefore was given much latitude in the legal texts in respect of the rates of interest and means of recovery as an incentive and transgression of the traditional rules such as on maximum accumulation came to be connived at, or partly legalised.

Like the mercantile community the Brahmins enjoyed a pre-eminence and acquired economic strength from the gifts of land and privileges.[20] The Brahmin writers on credit laws therefore attained their ingenuity to adjust the privileges of the highest caste with the rise of the lower order especially, Sudras. Laksmi elevates them in respect of food[21] and reserves certain articles like salt, milk, lac, hide, indigo, arms etc. as monopolies of the Sudras in trade, forbidding the Vaisyas to deal in these, while he allows money-lending to a Brahman in distress for the sake of his self and dependants. The artisan class including the distillers, basket-makers etc. came to enjoy the confidence of the investors in religious endowments. We find agriculturists, fishermen, shepherds, hunters and drummers making endowments individually or jointly. The position of women marked a definite improvement. The right of a widow to inherit an equal share with her sons in property was recognised in L.P. (p. 48) and in inscriptions. A

16. *Samaya* II 78.

17. *Rajat*. VIII 1990 f.

18. Chaturbhani II 24 : Upamitiabhava, p. 865—nidhanaka, p. 957—nidhi, p. 60.

19. *Uktivyakti*, Intro., p. 78.

20. D.C. Ganguli, *Paramaras*, p. 239, R. Niyogi, *Gahadavalas*, p. 217; N.S. Bose, *Chandellas*, p. 151.

21. B.P. Mazumdar, *Op. cit.*, p. 106.

daughter's right to mother's stridhan was preferred to a son's. The Dharmasastra tradition about their legal disability in being a witness or a party in transfer of immovable property e.g. by mortgage continued in theory only or in particular regions, for in the south we find a widow holding proprietary right over property and making over land and house to temple.[22] A lady became a member of the committee of justice (259 of 1909). The ascendancy of the courtesans was a part of the women's liberation in a permissive society. Vijnana's leniency about the caste of a courtesan (Y. II 290) reflects the social trend. Samaya (VIII 95 f) shows fleecing of merchants by a hetaira. The latter's social standing and economic status were at the peak in the Chola period. Devadasis made a number of endowments to temples and were married (147 of 1912, 411 of 1925). They not merely consorted with merchants but rose to be queens in Assam.[23] This was in consonance with the ascendancy of the mother cult and also reflected in the worship by Jains of the seven mothers near Ganesa and the Yaksini. All these created new resource pools in the pattern of endowment loaning.

Kinds of Loan and Interest

In this context, credit was expectedly directed more to unproductive than to productive purpose. Rajasekhara Suri[24] refers to gambling debt in a story where a Jain merchant released a prince from such debt. Smr. Cha. and Vya. Pra. refer to debt incurred for drinking (saurikam, surapanadinimittam) as an example of the avyavaharika debt; the latter explained it as not incurred for the benefit of relatives. Apararka explains it as that which is improper or unjustifiable[25] and Balambhatti as outside one's Vyavahara. It appears that vyavahara has not been used here in its technical sense of commercial dealings but maintenance of family which is taken as enough justification for contracting a debt. In the loan

22. *Ep. Rep.* of 1919, p. 80; no. 281 B of *S.I.I.* XII.
23. Cf. R. Dasgupta in *J.I.H.* Vol. 43 pt. 2.
24. Nanyayyam.
25. Svakaryavasat—p. 38.

bonds modelled in L.P., loans were contracted mostly by householders and formality required that necessity was to be written as the cause.[26] This was compatible with vyavahara of the Smrti texts. In Likh also loans were mostly taken for domestic urgency like a daughter's marriage (Letter no. 70). Ujjama tandula in Samaya matrka and grain loans in the bonds in Loka prakasa (pp. 15, 16) and L.P. (p. 21) prove that consumption loan occupied a large place in credit. The Samaya refers to housewives having borrowed rice. In L.P. (p. 21) the debtor borrowing paddy was a Nagara or merchant.

The stock phrase in L.P. about needs covered economic purposes also. Loans contracted by merchants (L.P. pp. 21, 23, 37-8, 42, 56), may be expected to have been contracted to serve economic rather than domestic purpose. A son borrowed 500 drammas from the merchant father out of his own share in ancestral property to be taken into account during partition for the purpose of investing the money in lending business. This may not be regarded as a case of loan strictly. It was a loan within the family and no interest was spoken of. It was not repayable before partition. The son's share in ancestral property was obviously treated as security. Was this ancestral property lying apart from that earned by the merchant father? Was the son entitled to father's property during the latter's lifetime? How could a share be given in security before it became due? Anyway, we get here a specific instance of securing money for investment in lending. In the *Likhanavali*, letter no. 71 records loans for investment in business. A *Kathasaritsagara* (p. 62) of story refers to a merchant who used to lend capital to poor men of good family to start with. He gave many *dinaras* to a person who could not preserve what he got. A boy sent by a teacher accepted from him a dead mouse as the capital, gave a receipt for it which was put in a strong box and engaged in a deal. The story of the mouse merchant reminds one of the Chullaka setthi/Jat. Borrowing at unusual rate of interest by traders who took great risk to earn greater profit was acknowledged

26. II. 78.

in Mita on Y. II 38. In Sukra much of the capital lent out is to be invested productively and the borrowers are entrepreneurs who seek temporary credit for expansion. While drawing up a rnapatra (II 623-4) the creditor is advised to satisfy himself that the debtor is capable of transacting business even on loans with interest (III 384-5). We have inscriptional evidence of advances being made by temple to cultivators or to assembly for irrigation to be noticed later. *Likhanavali* presents in letter no. 72 a loan for agricultural purpose.

Kinds of Interest

Of the six kinds of interest, Kayika was known to Govinda, Hardatta and Sarvajna in the same sense as to Medha (on M. III 153) i.e. bodily labour (Kayakarmasamsodhya). From Sarvajna it appears that service was to be rendered in lieu of interest only till the principal was not returned in the form it was received;[27] no time limit for the return or maximum period of service appears to be fixed. There is no textual confirmation of Vachaspati's view that Kayika was realised yearly. According to Mita, it was collected daily (pradidivasam grhyamana, on Y. II 37). Devana, Prthvi and Mitra take Kayika as interest from the physical benefit of cows or horses (dohana vahanadikah...vrddhitvena Kalpitah Smr. Cha. II 359). Madana-s. takes Kayika to be inclusive of the monetary interest if any paid in addition to the use of the animals.[28] This may not follow from the text in Vyasa but might have a basis in fact in this period. For in L.P. (pp. 19-20) we find that interest @ 2% (vyaja) p.m. was to be actually paid on a loan secured by pledging animals. These animals do not appear to be hypothecated but were at the disposal of the creditor, so that he would be in a position to sell them by intimating the debtor and the sureties, if payment in time failed, or in case of early foreclosure would add the cost of their maintenance to the total debt, as in such a case the cost of maintenance might be higher than any benefit as yet obtained. No one would like to spend on a pledge for no

27. On Manu, VIII 153.
28. p. 137.

benefit. Probably charging of interest over and above the use of pledge contravened law, so that a clause forbidding litigation is entered (Vadavivado rajakule na karyah). Vijnana, Devana and Mitra explain kalika as interest actually payable each month. In Maskarit (Gaut. XII 31) it is named Kalavrddhi and is to rise to 3 or 4 times the capital if payment in stipulated time failed. Kalluka supported by Raghava explains that a stipulated interest by monthly calculation should not be realised after the lapse of one year.[29] Sarvajna thinks that this referred to a mode of interest which makes the principal double in one year.[30]

Chanda thinks that the rule applies to a creditor who apprehends that his loan will be paid back too soon and to extend up to a period of one year only.[31] He refers to Halayudha's view that a creditor who wants to realise his interest before it ceases to accrue may have it before the lapse of one year. This shows that the interpreters strained their ingenuity to explain a rule that had become antique. Chanda approves it if only accepted by debtor and makes Karita subject to upward revision by experts in consideration of the risk involved. He also admits that sometimes the creditor receives compound interest by agreement. Sukra also was aware of this (633-34), like his predecessors Bhaskara introduces sums on interest. The significance of loaning of interest has been discussed in the genesis of compound interest. According to L. Gopal (p. 174), the sums in Bijaganita refer to such loaning of interest accrued. The sums IV 109 and 110 actually refer to reloaning of a part of the earlier loan, subtracting a square of the interest accrued from each sum.[32] This makes the new principal smaller than the earlier one in each case. This rather indicates the reluctance of a creditor to lend in an insecure situation. In each case however the rate of interest for the fresh loan was considerably

29. On Manu, VIII 153.
30. Ibid.
31. Vi. Ra. p. 9.
32. cf. Colebrooke, p. 194.

higher than in the earlier, at 10% instead of 5% in Vs. 109 and 5% instead of 1% in Vs. 110 p.m.

According to Chatterji (p. 34), Devana and other including Maskari (Gaut. XII 32) could not grasp the original significance of sikhavrddhi. Devana takes pratyaham gryhate to indicate the number of days in which a debtor promised to pay a debt. There is much confusion among the writers about the significance of adhibhoga in relation to Kayika. In Maskari it is a kind of daily interest such as in the form of ghee. Perhaps he meant this to be in addition to the use of pledge. Vachas understands bhogalabha to consist in the services rendered by slaves (pledged).[33] Kulluka notes the scope of a creditor's exaction in some of the types of interest by realising more than double in Kalavrddhi, overuse in Kayika and imposition of unusual rates in normal time in Karita. Sarvajna informs that the objectionable types of interest are not forbidden by some, while Govinda makes all types permissible for merchants, i.e. when loans are taken for economic pursuits.[34] It appears that the debt mechanism had become so sophisticated through centuries and operated in such a varied manner that each kind of interest known to the writers of different dates had developed subordinate forms all of which could not be comprised in the classification made.

Rates of Interest

The traditional rate of 1/80 or principal (i.e. 15%) has been upheld in Krtya (p. 217) and Vi. Ra. (pp. 446-7) on secured debts and 2% p.m. on the unsecured. 1/80 p.m. was advised by Madana-s. on loans for which no interest was stipulated or fixed by authorities as by Kat (505-6) on friendship loan if not returned after demand (5%). But this pious wish would not check arbitrary rates where these were not fixed beforehand. In most of the bonds in L.P. (pp. 20, 33, 34, 41, 42, 55) the rate is given as 2% p.m. It is found on loans secured with a pledge (p. 20) or not (p. 33). This departs from the Smrti

33. Dasadibhogah, Vi. Cha., 4.
34. Balkrishna, *Op. cit.*, p. 282.

provision of 3% on unsecured loan. The L.P. rate does not represent rates in operation but has been conventionally used. In grain loan the L.P. rate is 25% (Sapadika vardhamanah). If the date of return on Jyaisthi Purnima has any significance, then 25% for about a month is too high; but the loan date in every bond which has to fall on either Monday or Thursday in Baisakha is merely conventional. The rate 2% in Alberuni based on an idealistic report may similarly have been conventional. According to him, a Sudra was allowed to take percentages as long as his profit covered not more than 1/50 of the capital (II 150=Ch. 67). In L.Pr. we get various rates. On a short term grain loan 5 Khari was to be paid for 3 Khari in autumn (at a little less than the rate found in L.P. p. 21). Four per cent per month was charged on a money loan not secured by a pledge (L.Pr. p. 14) and 6% p.m. on another (p. 17) after an interest-free month in each case.[35] Another grain loan, if not paid in autumn after a month, was to increase probably at half interest of 4 to 5 prastha principle (according to our restoration). The present reading chatuh panchasikaya vrddhanuvrdhya is vague. Fiftyfour, an undefined figure, could not be the total payable on 10 Khari of grain for no time was fixed or known. There is no mention of periodicity e.g. month or year to make it a rate. Taken as chatuhpancha sikhaya, it makes vrddhyanuvrddhya understandable and tallies with Maskari's note on Gaut. XII 32 sikha dhanyasya yatha chaturanam prasthanam panchama. The same bond gives the standard measure of prastha (p. 18). The L.P. gives another instance of daily interest. On a loan pledged with horse (p. 18), if not paid within a short time, interest was to grow at 2% daily.[36] Horse-dealers (headaunagadena) with a prospect of high profit might agree to such demands of the creditor. On a loan secured with gold, 11% p.m. seems to be too high.[37] (2200 dinaras per month on di. 20,000). In Likha (Letter no. 68), 4 panas per tanka per month was quite high. Sukra in the Kautilyan spirit allowed

35. Ibid.
36. Ibid.
37. Compare 10% in year in L. Pr. (p. 19).

5% of profit as interest on capital for stock (cf. praksepa vrddhi). The upholders of law understood that high rates of interest must be allowed as an incentive to lenders who would otherwise be reluctant to lend in times of disturbances.[38] Transgressions of the prescribed rates came to be more and more convinced at. The rates in epigraphical (to be discussed later) and mathematical texts were in many cases higher and divergent.

In Bhaskara's Bijaganita, the rates of interest are seen to be 1, 2, 4, 5, and 10 p.c. p.m. 5% being in 4 out of 8 cases.[39] A sum similar to Bija Vs. 113 is presented in his Lilavati (Ch. IV. Sec. I Vs. 91)[40], which shows 5%, 3% and 4% on 3 portions of a capital. Vs. 89 gives 5%. The examples in Chap. III Vs. 80 and 81 show likewise 5% and about 4% respectively.[41] Here also 5% recurs in 3 out of 6 cases, and Lilavati shows 36% to 60% yearly.[42] The Ganitatilaka of Sripati mentions 2, 3, 4 and 5 per cent per month in the sums and repeats 5% in Vs. 98, 112, 114 etc. Vs. 114 shows certain extra charges payable along with interest (5%)—1 for futurity (bhavyaka), 1/2 dramma for profession (Vrtti) and 1/4 for the scribe (lekhaka). These texts thus reiterate 5% p.m. as the usual rate like some of their predecessors.

Differential Rates

Differential rates according to the risk involved in a business venture find favour in Mita (Y II 38) in view of the chance of the debtor's losing life and the capital. Twenty per cent per month is justified for fear of sinking of the capital. By Kantara the comm. understands not merely forest, deforestation being in progress, but any place hard to traverse where life and wealth might be at stakes.[43] In troublous period such places were not few and far between. So a creditor might demand

38. B.P. Mazumdar, *Op. cit.*, 221; L. Gopal, *Op. cit.*, p. 167.
39. Chap. IV Vs. 109—5% and 10%; Vs. 110—1% and 5%; Vs. 112—5%; Vs. 113—5%, 2%, and 4% on 390 lent in three portions.
40. S.C. Mukherji in *P.I.H.S.* 1958, p. 149.
41. Ibid.
42. Altekar, *Rastrakutas*, p. 374.
43. Ibid.

10% on loan for any business trip to a distant place. B.P. Mazumdar (p. 224) remarks that such high rates indicate that loans were advanced on personal security, for had there been other securities, no question of losing the principal would arise. It is not difficult to accept that some loans would be advanced without security but rates on such loans guarded with security might be profit-based (adhikalabhartham). It is strange that the above rates continued traditionally from Kautilyan times. Probably the scope of their application changed with time as evident from Medha and Vijnana. To a northerner sea voyage had less significance and Laksmi in the fashion of Medha understands by experts in a sea voyage, merchants in general (L. Gopal, p. 131).

Caste and Rates

The caste-graded rates had little practical value as has been observed. The personal credit of all Brahmins or of all Sudras could not be the same. The medieval scholiast could not get away from the notion of caste privilege held out by his authority. Devana and others accept to 5% rates in the absence of a pledge or surety. Vachaspati allows Vaisyas to charge 2·5% in normal times and creditors of other castes in distress. Sa. Vi.[44] bases the discriminatory rates on the creditor's caste as well more explicitly. He was to charge a debtor of his own caste interest at the flat rate of 24% and not at distinctional rate. A Brahmin creditor was to charge 36% from a Ksatriya, 48% from a Vaisya and 60% from a Sudra. A Ksatriya would charge 36% from a Vaisya and 48% from a Sudra. Thus a Sudra debtor would have to pay interest at different rates—60%, 48%, 36% and 24% according as the creditor was a Brahmin, a Ksatriya, a Vaisya or a Sudra, and a debtor would always prefer a creditor of his own caste. There is a lacuna as to the rates chargeable from debtors of higher castes than the creditor's own. The provision is unconfirmed and impracticable and only indicates that higher castes engaged in lending, if also a softening of the attitude towards distinctional rates (Sharma, p. 123).

44. Cf. Appadorai, *Econ. Con. in S. India*, I, p. 436.

On Commodities

The scholiasts dealt with different rates of accumulation on different commodities. Devana takes aksaya vrddhi stated by Vis. on flowers, fruits etc. as 100%. Chanda (Vi. Ra. 17-19) quotes both Kat and Br. on the maximum increase on commodities with no commitment and explains the contradictions on the basis of personal credit of the debtor and difference in time and place. Devana (Smr. Cha. II 373) adduces the need and solvency or poverty of a debtor as the ground, while Vijnana points out the capacity of a debtor as well as the general economic condition, indicating thereby that the accumulation rules should be applied after considering these things.[45] Others take one or other of the lines indicated. Different maxim may have been operative in different localities to which Smrti writers belonged, actual rates depending on the urge of either party in a transaction. The rates cannot be worked out in the absence of time limit of this accumulation. Derrectt applies the period of accumulation on cash loan @ 1/80 of principal p.m., i.e. 80 months to maximisation on commodities. Working of 2% p.m., Vivadarnavasetu takes this period to be 50 months. Chanda says that grain becomes double if paid in the next harvest (in two or three months) and becomes treble but not more if not paid at that time. This recalls a form of Kalika known to Maskari. Commentators do not record any change in maximisation that might have taken place in their own times to give us an idea of the supply position of particular commodities. For instance, one might expect a lowering of the maximum in respect of silk and metal which were in steady supply from foreign and indigenous sources in this period.[46]

The rule about maximum accumulation on cash was not observed in practice. Vijnana (Y. II 39) admits that more than double is realised when the interest is received every day or month or year and is not claimed in a lump.[47] Such relaxation

45. D.K. I. Pt. 2, 620.
46. *Manasollasa*, II Vs. 20-21.
47. *Vaijayanti*, p. 43.

accompanied needs of trade that revived in the period. Also in the case of transfer of a debt from one to another or a fresh transaction with the same debtor who pays less on the original debt (reka) or borrows more (seka), doubling limit is to be exceeded. Devana and others notice the practice of crossing this limit. Sukra upholds this limit in IV 631-32 but in V 192-93 remarks that if the creditor has obtained four times the principal, he is to receive no more.[48]

48. Vide, B.K. Sarkar, *S.B.H.*, V. 25, p. 108.

5

Deposit–Pledge–Surety–Recovery

(FROM 900-1200 A.D.)

Deposit

Terms for deposit used rather loosely show their different donations in different regions.[1] Vaijayanti (pp. 24, 124) makes nyasa, upanidhi, sthapya and niksepa synonymous. Ksirasvamin mentions upanidhi and nyasa as open deposit and niksepa as delivery of goods to a craftsman for making things. Mita (Y II 66, 67) and Vya. Pra. (p. 280) explain niksepa as deposit made (and counted ?) in the presence of a depositor, upanidhi as sealed (not counted) in his presence and nyasa as placed (counted or not) in the absence of the head of the family. To Visva nyasa was open deposit for safe custody and niksepa an article delivered for handing over to a third party. Niksepa is used for a deposit sealed with sign in Samaya (VIII 85, 87—sumudritam krtva). In Pra. Chin. nyasa (pp. 20, 95) implies a sacred trust not to be enjoyed and upanidhi (pp. 8-9, 108) as an ordinary deposit.[2] Many writers refer to deposits being made with merchants.[3] Merchant accepting deposits is mentioned as niksepavanik.[4] Samaya V 54 which actually refers to the request of a pledgor for the lessening of interest burden going unheeded may be stretched to mean

1. Ibid.
2. Ibid.
3. Ibid.
4. Naisadhiya III 43.

that the merchant turned deaf when approached for the release of a deposit as taken by L. Gopal (p. 178).[5] In Yasastilaka (49) the merchant friend of Bhadramitra denied a deposit made by the latter before sailing and claimed on return after losing merchandise in a shipwreck. References to merchants having embezzled deposits occur in Rajat. VIII 123 f., 706 f. It records an anecdote of a merchant deceit fully refusing a part with a deposit. Out of a deposit of 1 lakh of dinaras made with him 20 or 30 yrs. before, the depositor had drawn some amounts from time to time. When he claimed the balance, the merchant did not deny the deposit but made a counter demand placing an incredibly exaggerated account of the advances which he claimed as loans with interest. The case was settled in a suit and shows that peculation was common,[6] so that Kalhana makes a sweeping remark that a deposit made with a merchant is never recovered (VII 128). King Uchchala decided that as the deposit was not kept intact but had been used by the merchant he was also liable to pay interest on the same. This incidentally throws up a legal principle that a deposit of the open and counted type could by used by depositary and advaces could be drawn upon it; if used by depositary it became an interest-bearing debt; and the depositor was to pay interest on the advances drawn, which is however open to doubt. Kat's provision (505-6) for 5% p.m. interest on a deposit if not returned on demand probably became theoretical whence this embezzlement.

In Vi. Ra. (pp. 86-7) a depositary incurs no blame if he uses an unsealed deposit for sometime and then replaces it. Naradatta (on Gaut. XII 39) exempts a bailee's son from liability for loss or misappropriation of a deposit. If a deposit be lost in accident or taken by thieves or a king, it need not be returned. In periods of trouble many such deposits would be plundered or taken by king for reasons of state. Such concessions were allowed to a bailee in order to encourage him to accept deposits or even use it in business (including lending ?) in disturbed conditions. Nidhiniksepa mentioned among the

5. Ibid

6. Stein, Tr. note on Vs. 123.

taxes in Kamauli Grant (V.S. 1230) is taken to denote a tax imposed by the Gahadavala Govt. on property held in trust.[7] If this be correct one has to guess again which party was to pay this tax, the depositor or the depositee. L. Pra. (p. 29) presents a receipt for niksepa given by a depositee acknowledging to return it whenever wanted back with a reference to mahajana and witness.

Pledge

Commentators have tried to explain adhi and bandhaka derivatively.[8] Adhi is placed with a creditor for inspiring confidence. (Mita, Y.II 58), and bandha is taken as a pledge kept with a common friend (Smr. Ch. II 318, Vya. Pra. 224-5). While according to Prthvi (p. 204) bandha was a pledge for custody only and adhi of the usufructuary type, Chanda (p. 5) thinks both of them to be usufructuary. According to Jagannath, bandha was abbogya or non-usable (Col. Dig. I 17). Bandha in certain cases may refer to hypothecation without a physical transfer of the article to the creditor, it sometimes being kept with a third party, who might be a particular kind of surety. Hypothecation without possession is held out in a document in L.P. (p. 21). 25 measures of wheat were to be paid after threshing season for a loan of 20 measures. This indicates that a charge was created upon the standing crop of the field though it was not lying under the creditor's possession. In L.P. (38 grhadulipatram) interest was to be paid, though a house was pledged, probably this was not according to vrddhiphalabhogachara. Hypothecation without possession was known to Kat (cf. Kane, 431) and Nilakantha. According to the latter, the debtor gives an undertaking (nirbandha) that he will not alienate the bandha by sale, gift or mortgage so long as the debt is not paid.[9]

7. R. Niyogi, *The Hist. of the Gahadavala Dyn.*, p. 172. Others take it in the sense of treasure-trove.
8. H. Chatterji, 212 f.
9. Vya. Ma P. 166.

Kinds of Pledge

As to the kinds of pledge, Mita (Y II 64) refers to the sapratyaya and apratyaya types of bhogyadhi of Br under the name savrddhikamulapakaranarthah, where from the income of a pledge both principal and interest were to be realised, and vrddhimatrapakaranarthah where enjoyment was in lieu of interest only. It accepts the name ksayadhi for the first type as appropriate. Sa. Vi. (p. 942) mentions two other names for this type—paribhasitadhi and samvidadhi. Para. Ma (174) shows various subdivisions of adhi. Sa. Vi refers to pratyaya bhogyadhi of the earlier authorities and pertinently remarks that there may be an inter-mixture of different types according to the terms of agreement (pp. 233, 234, 244). It says that a bhogyadhi may be transformed into a gopyadhi after enjoyment for a stipulated period even though the capital is not returned by that time. It refers to Khandadhi as a pledge to secure a principal along with its interest for a stipulated period which generally ends in a sale. The value of a pledge for custody might not cover the principal and its interest in special cases, e.g. in charitrabandhaka. A debtor being known to be very honest, a property of small value may be given as security for a large debt, or the creditor being known to be very honest, a property of greater value for a small loan may be placed as pledge (Mita, YII 61). These are exceptional. In satyahkara there is a promise to pay double but the thing pledged was not to be lost. Mita (Y II 64) explains that the enjoyment of a pledge may continue beyond the doubling point, if capital is not paid. It adds that if the income from a mortgaged property falls short of the stipulated interest the balance has to be paid by debtor along with the principal during redemption. Smr. Cha. II 344 expresses perhaps the same view and says that a debtor cannot redeem a pledge in a specified time by paying the principal only, if the income from a pledge minus necessary expenses, does not cover the total interest expected. In L.P. (36-7) where a house was mortgaged and to be used by the creditor, no interest was charged. Here the interest was co-extensive with the rent of the house.[10]

10. Ibid.

According to A.K. Majumdar,[11] this indicates that in villages money was more difficult to get than in a town where no further interest besides the benefit from a pledge was charged. The case was slightly different with a horse-dealer who, though having an access to towns contracted a loan in a village (Valua game, L.P. 41) by pledging horses and could afford to pay interest at that; the rate in such a case in L.Pr. 18 was very high. The urge to borrow and paying capacity made the difference.

If the mortgage got damaged in any manner, the mortgagee could get it repaired and add the cost to the original sum.[12] If the house is destroyed by natural calamity or accident the mortgagor was to replace it. If he was unable to do so, the creditor was to get it built and have the cost entered as an interest-bearing loan in the document intimating the debtor.[13] No corresponding clause occurs protecting the interests of the debtor in case any mortgaged animal died due to creditor's negligence. The L.P. documents urge the debtor to replace (p. 41) pledged animals in case of their death for reasons beyond control, or to bear the brunt of their suffering (p. 20) whereas in L.Pr. (19) if a horse died half the value was to be borne by the creditor.[14] This recalls Jagannatha's practical solution by apportioning the loss of a pledged animal between the debtor and the creditor to avoid quarrel.[15] Mita confirms the debtor's responsibility in replacing a pledge lost for no fault of the creditor's. If however a house got damaged due to mortgagee's violating the clauses forbidding its use as a store for grain, gram or salt, then he was to bear the charges of repair. If an adhi be destroyed at creditor's fault and not restored, he will lose the capital and also the interest if there be any (Mita, Y.II 59); Vijnana's references to an interest in the case of bhogyadhi indicate that he was

11. *Chalukyas of Gujarat*, pp. 278-9.
12. L.P., 37.
13. Ibid.
14. Ibid.
15. Col. Dig I. 116.

aware of interest being taken over and above the user.[16] Smr. Ca. II 324 shows a sympathetic attitude to the pledge in the case of adverse possession and loss of a pledge and does not support total forfeiture of capital. Mita holds that a pledge acquires ownership over a pledge only after the expiry of time limit. Devana argues that the debtor loses his ownership over the pledge after the time limit including the grace period of two weeks. The deed of mortgage which contains a clause as to the lapse of a pledge after a given period or doubling of loan becomes a sufficient instrument for the transfer of ownership. The question of ownership has vexed the minds of the commentators and contrary extent of the amount due only, for if the pledge be of greater value, the balance out of the sale proceeds has to be returned to the debtor or his heir (Smr. Ch. II 333). In some of the L.P. deeds there is express stipulation that the creditor could sell the chattel or property for the whole or a part of the debt not paid on or before a specified date (e.g. Aksayatrtiya, p. 37, Dipotsava, p. 38). It was to be sold at the best possible price in the open market like vegetables (sakapanikanyayena or khanda vadara nyayenavikriya dramma grahitavyah). He could sell the pledge only after informing the debtor and the sureties (dharanika pratibhuvam viditam, p. 20) and could charge the debtor or the sureties for shortage if any (pp. 20, 40, 41). A debtor, even if he brought the money in full on the day following the specified, would not be allowed to redeem. This shows that the grace period was not always allowed in practice, and depended on the creditor's discretion.

If a creditor in straitened circumstances wanted to have his capital back before the stipulated period he would approach the debtor for recovery in the company of bhattaputras and adhipalas bhattaputranutavesya. The bhattaputras might me judicial officers (cf. A.K. Majumdar, p. 280) and their expenses were to be borne by the debtor. If upavesya here suggests acharita, meaning warrior band (cf. ed. Dalal and Shrigondekar, Gloss) standing for goonda elements may be accepted. Redemption of land from an

16. Ibid.

unwilling creditor is recorded in an insc. from the south probably of the Haysala period. The creditor Diksit Naganna, who also seems to be a Brahmin, did not return the pledge document to Somagauda of Mattigatta who returned the debt with interest. The discharge of the debt was therefore inscribed in the presence of the mahajanas of the village.[17] This recalls a provision of Kautilya and some jurists. Mita insists on the return of document after repayment. L.P. (37) provides that if a creditor wants to recover his loan in distress and if the debtor is unable to pay, the former can transfer the document to another creditor and take the money from him. But the debtor must be informed of this previously (or the new creditor should be known to him).[18] This follows as an alternative of recovery from the debtor. The phrase na va means here 'failing that', 'alternatively' or 'otherwise' and does not forbid transfer as taken by some.[19] They presume the existence of this right of the creditor from the absence of its prohibition in another document (L.P. 36-7). Rather from L.P. it appears that this right was not to be ordinarily exercised unless specifically allowed as in the document (p. 37). This right came to be recognised by legal experts rather late. Kulluka admits this custom as prevailing in many regions.[20] Devana seems to recognise this practice but discourages sub-pledging for a sum greater than the principal (Smr. Ch. II 3 3). Madhava refers to this as vastvadhi which may be allowed only after the principal has reached double with interest and may be done earlier by mutual consent.[21] Vijanana and Chanda do not favour this practice. Both sub-mortgage and re-mortgage are linked to the ownership question. In Smr. Ch. II 340, transfer of a pledge by the pledgor is considered weak as his ownership is obstructed by pledge. Vi. Ra. 621 thinks on the authority of Halayudha that as pledge

17. Ibid.
18. A.R. Mysore Arch. Dept. no. 29, p. 38.
19. Ibid.
20. Cf. Majumdar, *Op. cit.*, 227.
21. On Manu VIII 143.

is weaker than sale, the pledgor could sell it, the pledge not being entitled to any share. Mita, Y II 23 does not favour remortgage and though this is done out of avarice, the first done will prevail in a conflict of transactions. In a clash of possession and document or other evidence, it (on Y II 60) loans on possession as contributing validity to a pledge. Devana also is on the aids of possession, noting the exceptions like Medha that when the pledgee has to stay away absence of possession should not weaken a pledge. In case of interrupted possession, the evidence of witnesses was important according to Jagannatha.

House mortgage was common in Gujerat as indicated by L.P. (pp. 36-7, 38, 42; more deeds were added later, pp. 70, 76). The particulars e.g. boundaries were always recorded as urged in Kat. (522) to make mortgage valid. The boundaries of a house are not given (p. 38) probably because it was pledgor's residence hypothecated. Pledging of cattle was common in village and was an easy means of raising funds by cultivators and cattle-dealers who had to pay both Kayika and Karita interest simultaneously. L. Pr. (p. 18) and Likh (let. 76) show the same. Grain was given in pledge along with gold ornaments in L. Pr. (21). Gold bullion given in pledge for custody is known as bandha to Jagannatha (kanchanapindah). It is abhogya in the sense that it is impaired by use. There is a document on land mortgage in L.P. (39). The land mortgaged by Somagauda mentioned above was Vrtti land. Mortgage or sale of gift land was generally forbidden (nadheyam na cha vikreyam, p. 118, Puri Pls of Ramachandra, S. 1232). Utter distress or withdrawal of state patronage can account for such alienation. The payment of interest raises doubt as to in whose possession the pledge was lying. If the pledgor retained possession, this provides an epigraphic evidence of hypothecation. Jaunpur Brick Ins. (1217 A.D.)[22] records that Gangadeva borrowed 2250 sadboddika drammas from two creditors (joint) on the security of cultivated lands (pravapini) in his own share (svakapattika) and attested signature. It does not refer to interest probably because the land was to be enjoyed by the

22. *Para. Ma.* 182—III p. 242 (Kane).

mortgagee. The mortgage of land to temple or by temple to an individual are to be discussed under temple inscriptions.

Surety

While defining suretyship, Vijanana followed by some others lays emphasis on confidence that a third party inspires in a creditor for a transaction (on Y II 53—Visvasartham). The names of sureties must occur in a bond even in a loan taken one's father (L.P., 56). The importance of sureties for recovery was stressed in the L.P. bonds. They were to be informed before sale of a pledge by creditor (pratibhuvam viditam, p. 20). If the sale proceeds did not cover the whole debt including interest and incidental expenses then the rest was to be paid by the sureties by borrowing on interest from other creditors or selling their own movables. If any of the pledged chattels died in accident or the like, the sureties with the debtor remain liable and should not enter into any dispute with the creditor. They also were to bear the charges for employing bhattaputras for recovery. Abandoning all complaints the adhipalaka pratibhu was to effect the recovery of the debt with interest and all expenses. Majumdar's view (pp. 280-1) that adhipalas were village arbitrators is not convincing, as their names appear in the place of sureties; village elders are not expected to endorse each pledge deed and remain liable for recovery. The adhipalaka pratibhu (p. 21) does not seem to be a dvandva compound and was known to Har. and Pita. (qu. Smr. Ch. II 350) as a special type of surety who was responsible for handling over a pledge to the creditor, if he was holding it himself or if it had not been delivered by a debtor or else to pay himself. L. Gopal (p. 164) has shown by comparing the L.P. documents (pp. 37, 41 etc.) that they were guarantors and liable for payment. It is repeatedly stated that each of the sureties was to consider himself as the debtor, which was in keeping with the definition by commentators (tadvad bhavati).[23] It also states that though there may be many sureties they were responsible jointly and

23. *J.U.P.H.S.* XVIII 196; *J.A.S.B.* XIX 454.

severally.[24] Any one might be approached and was liable to pay whatever was due if others kept silent. The word danaya occurs before pratibhu (p. 37) and raksapala appears in pp. 36, 56, little distinction being made between such appellations. Likh (let. 61) sets out 3 types of surety, darsaka lagnaka (for appearance), pratyeka lagnaka (for recovery) and datr lagnaka (for payment). The classification tallies with that in Mita (Y II 55) and Sukra (IV 5. 125-6). Pramana pratibhu in Smr. Ch. II 347 like vivadapratibhu had functions in a court. Bhunjapaka and pratyarpaka were sureties responsible for delivery of a pledge for use to the creditor and debtor respectively. Surety for confidence who certifies the bonafides of a debtor (Mita—Y II 53, Smr. Ch. II 346) might be called for in apprehension of evil intentions of a debtor (Vi. Ra. 4 42-3). Devana betrays confusion in interpreting upasthana sometimes in delivery of pledge to creditor, though actually it refers to surety for appearance.[25] He misinterprets niradistadhana, who receives money from debtor according to Medha, as a wealthy surety for appearance also liable for payment. Jagannatha in the light of much later juridical developments limits the responsibility of a surety for confidence to the extent of his certificate, while the responsibility of surety for payment remains. Rnidravyarpana has been taken differently by different commentators (Chatterji, p. 117 f.) according to their knowledge or probably the real sense was lost. Vi. Chin. 14 lays stress on the competence of a surety. A person on whose death realisation of money may become uncertain should not be accepted as a surety (Vi. Ra. 39). Special relationship with either of the parties renders a surety unsuitable. Mita (Y. II 52) accepts undivided brother being a surety by mutual consent. In Jaunpur Br. Ins., the surety is called on apta.[26] According to Ballantyne (J.A.S.B. XIX 454), he was to be "one as a king might be content with"; V.S. Agarwala (J.U.P.H.S. XVIII 196) thinks that he was to be

24. Vijnana Y II 10, Nanda—Vis. VI 21, Bhaudsvami, N.M.S I 101.
25. Ibid.
26. Cf. H. Chatterji, pp. 153-4, 181; Vys Pra., 244; also padadarsi in Maskari in Gaut. XII 38.

bound with such conditions as may be enforced by the king (rajoparohena). It is possible that the surety took the risk of paying another man's debt relying on the Smrti provision of getting double or even more in case of commodities from the debtor (Majumdar, 0.283). Vijnana (Y. II 56) is opposed to his making paying in a hurry to get this benefit. He identifies such dues to the surety with a friendship loan not to carry interest before demanded as laid down in Kat. (505) and questions the propriety of his getting double. Devana supports his getting double on the strength of authority (vachanabalat—Smt. Ch. II 357). The embarrassment of a surety to pay the debt of an absconding debtor by selling the latter's land is recorded in an insc. (503 of 1926).

Names of witnesses occur in inscriptions and loan bonds. As many as five endorsed a document (L.P. 21). Witness testified let. no. 68 in Likh. Witness evidence was to be considered sufficient in case a document was lost (Sukar IV 637-8) or letters get mudged or obliterated (Jaunpur Br. Insc.).

The L.P. asserts that even if something is deleted or inserted, the deed remains authoritative. This perhaps impairs the sacrosanct character of a document. False documents might be performed taking advantage of debtor's illiteracy. There is no indication that deeds were registered. The Jaunpur brick bears no such stamp.[27] Somagauda's inscription was made in the presence of village elders. Promissory note was known as kayeluttolai.

An attempt to classify the bonds under different names has been made in the L.P. though not very satisfactorily. Vyavaharapatra (p. 55) though little different was an acknowledgement by debtor in the first person. So were svahastaksarani (p. 56) and sammukha hastaksarani (p. 55) and in each case there were sureties. Thus the presence or absence of sureties cannot be a point of difference as seems to have been made.[28] The difference between adhipatra and adhau

27. Ibid.

28. Nothing is known of the two such documents on copper in the possession of Cap. Kittoe, J.A.S.B. XIX (1850), p. 451.

krtavastunam upari grhita dravya may be that the former was a mortgage of immovable (house) and the latter of movable (cattle) property. The name danakapatra was applied to a pledge of horse (p. 39), house (p. 37) and field (p. 39), it being called asvaddanaka or ksetraddanaka as the case might be. Graddabaja was perhaps the same as vrddhiphalabhogapatra (p. 36) and little different from grhaduli. Both in danaka and duli, the house mortgaged was to lapse to the creditor. The only difference may be that while an interest was payable in the case of grhaduli, possession was in lieu of interest in the other; whether possession was given to the creditor by grhaduli is not clear, probably it was not. In valitapatra a garden was mortgaged to clear unpaid debt with interest from its income (p. 34). This was the same as sapratyaya bhogyadhi with the difference that the mortgage was performed after the accumulation of a debt. Vrddhi dhanyaksarani was for a grain loan without a pledge. It may be that in the loan deeds named aksarani, the letters of the document were of supreme importance, as there was no pledge, except perhaps in the case of the loan from one's share in ancestral property might be a kind of security. In Samaya, ujjamapatrika (VIII 96) was the same as dhanadharana patrika (ib. 95) or adhikarana patra (Ibid. 104) in promise or acknowledgement of a sum (pratyayahetu), Ibid. 95; the harlot was insisting on its performance by a merchant's son. Ujjama chirikas meant deeds in acknowledgement of debts. Stein notes that ujjama was a Skt. original (or version) of uzum (=debt) in Kashmir.[29] In L. Pr.[30] it occurs along with dinara, dhanya or bandha (e.g. dinarojjama chirika and so on) for cash, grain or mortgage loans. The work distinguishes chirika from hundika though no such distinction has been observed in the examples that follow under arthipratyarthi pattakam. The term hundika like ujjama was of late origin and means bill of exchange. It comes dinara, dhanya yavagodhuma, sevya

29. Cf. A.K. Majumdar, p. 28?; L. Gopal, p. 170.

30. Stein on ujjama dhanam in Rajat VIII 1?7.

(=wine of medicine), gotika nama etc. (e.g. dinara-hundika and so on).[31]

Damodra has named the fifth prakarana in liktivyakti as Vyavaharika lekhapatra likhanakrama. He lays down that a document should begin with the names of king, date (tithi, day, year etc.) and place and record the names, fathers' names, castes etc. of creditor, debtor, surety (madhyaka), witness and scribe (if father is alive—Jivatpitrkasya) and then the amount and interest. Signature should precede and mention of the scribe (Vs. 42-45). The author promises to illustrate varieties of lekhapatra, panjikopagatapatta-chiraka and bhundika (=hundika?) but a, unfortunately that portion has not come to our hand, no comparison can be made with the loan bonds otherwise known. Vidyapati's Likh deals with similar loan deeds current in Mithila in a later period. All these amply increased use of letters of credit by traders and house-holders which was due not so much to a security of coins as to insecurity on roads.

Transformation of an unpaid debt with interest into a principal in a renewed bond has been supported by Mitra. Devana indicates that this contingency arises to allow the interest to grow further. As explained in Mita (Y. II 39), an amount less than the old debt, a part having been paid or a concession made by creditor (reka), or a greater amount including a further advance (seka)[32] might be made the principal in a new bond. The case in L.P. (34-5) was basically not a novation of an unpaid debt to grow interest but a mode of payment. It was no doubt made after 3C0 dram had grown to 600 (double). For the total debt including interest a garden was given in pledge not merely as a security but in realisation of the debt from the income. As it was to yield 100 dram a year, the pledge was to enjoy it for six years only. It resembles sapratyayabhogyadhi but made long after a loan had been

31. P. Niyogi, Ec. His. N. Ind., p. 277, gives the impression that the terms occur in the Rajat referring to Stein, Tr. Vol. II. p. 313, but Stein refers to the Lokaprakasa.

32. B.P. Mazumdar, *Op. cit.*, pp. 223-4, quotes a bond L. Pr. (p. 19), also App. B. below.

received. Incidental expenses incurred for the maintenance of a pledge were entered in the bond to be realised during payment in L.P. documents. It does not appear that such sums were added to principal to yield interest. Part payments made by debtors if not the back of the bonds or receipt were to accrue interest as a measure against creditor's motive of receiving payment twice (Vi. Ra. p. 81). In final settlement a debt was to be paid before the same witnesses (Mita on Y. II 94) or in their absence before others (Smr. Ch. II 377). Almost all the deeds in L. Pr. end with a clause—yasya haste-yam hundika tasyaivam—which may mean that the debtor acknowledged to pay the bearer or anybody to whom the hundika might be transferred. A market of salable bonds emerged in rather an advanced economic stage. Some bonds in L. Pr. conclude with a clause that the hundika was not redeemable or valid after 10 yrs. (p. 17) or 8 yrs. (p. 18). The time limits for calling in a hundika might have been set to check a creditor's motive to wait too long for an increase and to activise the parties in the possibility of evasion in keeping with Smrti provision.

Non-payment and usurpation increased in a disturbed condition, and methods of recovery became harsh. Sukra (IV 635-6) advises the king to interfere whenever a person though not incapable does not pay back. Sovadi Ins. of Chahamana Ratnapala (1176 V.S.)[33] record the admonition that a non-payer goes to hell.

Recovery

Dharma method consisting in persuasion with sweet words about merit in returning other's thing (cf. Sarvajna) and demerit in usurpation (cf. Nanda) was seldom effective. Smr. Ch. (II 383) enlarges the scope of chhala method by understanding other things as well in the device of holding up anvahita deposit (from anvahitadi). Acharita as fasting at debtor's door was known to the commentators. Chanda includes confinement of the debtor's family (putradararodha,

33. *Ibid.*

Vi. Ra. 68). Katha sa. (LV 5, 3.5) refers to a similar practice.[34] It has been observed that in recovery of debt a Brahmin might be employed to perform acharita and even distraint in a safe and effective manner by dint of his immunity and highness.[35] The Nadole Ins. (1198 V.S.) refers to fasting into death by Brahmins to make a king relent.[36] Rajat also refers to this practice by Brahmin.[37] Detention by force could be performed by the creditor himself or by some other person employed on remuneration according to local custom (Smr. Ch..II 384).[38] The rude person employed used to be ruder to make the debtor pay, as his remuneration was to come with the debt-money thus realised. Upaniti remarks on the plight of debtors in confinement by cruel creditors.[39] It was indeed hard to get out of their clutches without making full payment. There is a dialogue in Uktivyakti[40] from which appears that in Kanyakubja (perhaps also in Benares) the merchant lenders used to maintain private jails where to confine defaulters, who could be released by paying money taken from a friend. Such a person preferred a forest infested with snakes and tigers to a residence near an evil soul.

Hemachandra in Dvyasraya Kavya[41] (III 40) uses a simile which suggests that for an unpaid sum the debtor used to be taken to a river bank and bound with a chain or rope by the creditor. Exposed to the scorching rays of the sun, he failed to reach the waters and resembled a tortoise. Abhayatilaka Gani comments that these creatures are found on the river bank in autumn. A. K. Majumdar (p. 284) surmises that debts were usually settled before or during autumn. This is borne out by the loan bonds and probably autumn was a harvest time when grain loans especially were to be paid back.[42]Another

34. E.I. XI 313, 1.59.60.
35. Ibid.
36. Hopkins, J.A.O.S. XXI, 146 f.
37. E.I. XI 37.
38. IV—by Brahmani; VIII 709, VII 1088—by parisadiya Brahmanas, etc.
39. Ibid.
40. Ibid.
41. Karika 29, p. 23 1.15 f.
42. Ibid.

custom that seems to be less harsh and claims an antiquity has been mentioned by foreign writers. To attest the integrity of the Indians Al Idrisi[43] says that when a man has a right to demand anything of another and happens to meet him he has only to draw a circular line upon the ground and to make his debtor enter it, which the latter never fails to do, and the debtor cannot leave this circle without satisfying his creditor or obtaining the remission of the debt. This has been reiterated by Marco Polo (II 343),[44] Kaswini and Varthena. Though traced in Mrchchha, the practice would be of doubtful effect, especially when a debtor who possessed nothing had only a line to cross to escape. This probably was a garbled version (cf. Majumdar, p. 284) of the application of bala or was a mixture of bala and acharita so that it finds no mention in the Smrtis. If the bhattaputras in L.P. had been introduced to effect recovery by distraint, it would mean sale of debtor's chattels other than the pledge. But Vijnana was opposed to sale of debtor's land not pledged.[45]

As to realisation of debt through service he (on Y. II 43) likes of not being employed by a creditor of lower caste. He takes Brahmanas to stand for any superior caste and by implication exempts Ksatriyas and Vaisyas from serving the creditor when he was a Sudra, thus limiting considerably the scope of debt servitude. The scope is slightly enlarged by subjecting a debtor to the service of a creditor of his own caste, a Brahmin being no exception, when he comments that in the rule lower caste is also indicative of equal caste but then he qualifies saying that the nature of the service must be agreeble to the debtor's etc. and without detriment to the interest of his family. This limitation of the scope of exploiting a debtor's labour though reflecting a rise of the lower orders could not wipe out the social malaise which was noticed by N. Conti.[46]

43. Vartamana saradi, L.Pr., p. 16; Kartikante, L.P., p. 34.
44. Eliot and Dowson, I (pub. S. Gupta), p. 122: Tr. by Jaubert. Nainar, Arab Geographers, etc., 97.
45. According to a note by Caldwell, this was attended with warnings of course if the line was crossed without making payment.
46. Cf. Sharma, Light etc. p. 135.

Vyavahar is understood as legal proceedings by many commentators except Chanda who equates it with detention of debtor in public (Vi. Ra. 67). They also deal with the penalty for unnecessary litigation in case of a debtor once denying and then admitting a claim or a rich debtor reluctant to pay. They have little to say about the penalty for a dishonest creditor. In the L.P. documents the debtors and sureties are repeatedly asked not to quarrel with the creditor or to file a suit in which case they would have to bear all the expenses as the defeated party.[47] No such warning against a creditor's malafides does occur. Was this a pious wish to lessen the chance of useless litigation, or would a suit come to be dismissed on the strength of this clause? Rajat. VIII 123, 129 and 149 f. refer to debt suit relating to an embezzled deposit. When judges were unable to decide, King Uchchala settled the case in favour of the plaintiff, making the depositee liable to pay interest on a used-up deposit. Though no reference was made to a Smrti text in support, the sentence was in keeping with Kat's provision. There is no reference to a surety or witness or bond. The deposit (open) was called in for inspection. A coin bearing the name of the present king was shown for the deposit made in the reign of a past king. This was sufficient proof for the use of the deposit without the depositor's knowledge. The mere replacement of the deposit was not enough to exclude interest due to its use.

With reference to the priority of a debt to srotriya[48] in repayment, Devana takes it to denote a Brahmin and not all Dvijas conversant with Vedas. This was perhaps in recognition of the urgency of royal dues, the Brahminical superiority complex persisting. In case of debts contracted on the same date he holds up two principles of repayment in inadequacy of fund—in proportion to the debt amounts and with preference for a debt utilised to earn the assets.[49] L.P. (20) shows that in the creditor's absence or demise the loan assets were to be paid to his heirs or coparceners.[50]

47. Major, India, p. 31.
48. Ibid.
49. Cf. Kane, II pt. 1, p. 143 f.
50. Also L.P. (21).

The same document thus stresses the liability of the sons and grandsons of a debtor. Alberuni observes that 'the debts of the deceased must be paid by his heir, either out of his share or of the stock of his own property, no regard being had whether the deceased has left any property or not' (II 164, Ch. LXXII). From his reference to Manu it may be surmised that his information was based on ancient Smrti tradition rather than on actual conditions. Vijanana and Devana make it explicit that sons and grandsons are ipso facto liable for a debt inheriting property or not.[51] They agree with Mitra[52] that if a grandson does not inherit property he was liable to pay the principal only. Physical and legal incompetence exempts a son (Smr. Ch. II 394-5). An able son was not to pay certain debts (immoral). Certain types of surety-debts were reckoned as within a son's obligation but without interest while grandsons were totally exempt (Smr. Ch. II 352, Vi. Ra. 44). Debts contracted for the joint family were binding upon the coparceners. The father was responsible for a debt so made by the son (Y. II 45) but not for the latter's personal debt, though his personal debt was binding on the son. A woman was to pay such debts if she inherited property and if not only the sahakrta and abhyupeta debts of her husband out of stridhana but not his immoral debts.[53] Ordinarily a husband was not liable for wife's personal debt but conjugal liability arose wherever subsistence depended on mutual earnings (Mita Y II 48; Vi. Ra. 60). Yosidgraha or one who accepts another's wife as his own (punarbhu and svairini) was liable to pay the first husband's debts but not one who merely enjoys such a woman. The distinction brings in relief a woman's remarriage in a section of the society in spite of sastric disfavour (Mita, Y II 51, Smr. Ch. II 404-5). Marriage of courtesans is established by epigraphy.

51. Smr. Ch. II 391-2.

52. L.P. (20).

53. Pitradhanabhave-pi—Mita, Y II 50; pitrdravyagrahance-pi—Smr. Ch. II 395; cf. L. Gopal, p. 161, on inheritance as a condition.

Usury

A change in the attitude towards money-lending is evident in the law books, which might be due to the needs of a society in economic expansion, but harvests often failed and unsettled conditions shakened the confidence of lenders. Sukra places the services of capital and labour to society on the same footing and does not condemn lending.[54] It is not considered immoral in Mita (I 119, II 39). It defines Kusida[55] as Vrddhyartham dravyaprayogah and vardhusa as a usurer taking prohibited interest.

Interest taking has been praised by Laksmi as the best means of acquiring wealth.[56] Garuda praises it if not with a sneer[57] as the safest of all ways. Whereas agriculture is hampered by drought, disturbances, rats etc., usury thrives in all seasons, day or night. The usurer earns profit staying home, for which a trader has to travel wide.[58] Condemnation of the usurer no doubt recurs (Krtya-Grha 215-6, Vi. Ch. p. 2—atipidakaratvat), his food being untouchable and sin most heinous. But Garuda presents the expiation rites by propitiating Brahmins and the manes with a part of the profit. The same text permits Brahmanas and Ksatriyas to practise lending in distress and through other persons in normal times.[59] Mita (Y.III 42) and Vi.Chi (3) agree on this. Even the poor were not exempt from the exaction of Bramin usurers.[60] Alberuni who says that only a Sudra was allowed to take interest was probably guided by the scriptural ban on this pursuit for a Brahmana. The sin, he reports, 'which a man commits thereby' corresponds to the amount by which the percentages have

54. Vys-Pra. 264.
55 G.T. Deshpande criticises Vijanana's approach to the issues in Y. II 45, 46, 51, Idol. papers I, p. 181 f.
56. Cf. B.K. Sarkar, Ib., p. 107.
57. Cf. Haradatta, Kuserumbhomedeta, etc.
58. Ibid.
59. Cf. K.V.R. Aiyanger, *Aspects of Anc. Ind. Econ. Thought*, p. 50. Curiously Kusida is appended after bhaiksya as one of the ten livings.
60. Garuda 215, ref. in Vachaspatyam; Chap. 229, p. 721 in Tr. M.N. Dutt.

increased the capital stock.[61] Generally speaking, the lending-business was a part of the occupation of the merchants. The four chief occupations which attracted the merchant in Gujerat was shipping, trade (especially in cloth), jewellery and banking.[62] One of merchant's four sons declaring in succession their adopted vocations preferred lending.[63] Uktivyakti also identifies merchant as the lender.[64] In Jaunpur Br. Ins., the creditors are called dhanika (merchant) where two brothers, Brahma and Mahaditya, invest in lending jointly, showing that joint venture was not uncommon. In L.P. the creditor was invariably a dhanika called a vyavaharika (voharika of Pali literature). Both in the inscription and the L.P., the deeds begin saying that the creditor invests his own money to earn profit (labhaya svadhanam prayumkta). The instance of merchant's son borrowing from father to invest in lending (Vyavahararatham, p.56) has been found in L.P. It may thus appear that money-lending was identified with a distinct section of the society. But differentiation was far from complete, and even house-holders engaged in lending in some form or other. Uktivyakti alludes to money-lending as a common practice.[65]

The income of a creditor was taxable according to Sukra (IV 2, 255, Sarkar, ib. p. 149), where the usurers were to pay 1/32 of the interest gained to the state. This presupposes that the conspicuous bankers were registered in a state department which maintained an account of their visible income. This lacks confirmation.[66] The creditors' dues are taken into account (and paid up?) during the partition of the deceased debtor's property (L.P. 47).

A usurer is painted with a black brush by the Kashmirian writers as being uncouth both physically and by nature. In

61. Cf. Prayaschittavivekah.
62. Cf. M. R. Majumdar, *Cultural Hist. of Gujerat*, p. 186.
63. Sachao II 50—Ch. LXVII.
64. Cf. Samalabhat's Vidyavilasini.
65. Brhat Kavya dohana III 243.
66. Ibid.

Samaya (VIII 53 f)[67] a merchant creditor is recognised by being seated in shop, turning *blind* as soon as seeker arrives, *deaf* when approached by a debtor for the release of mortgage with a request for remission of interest and *dumb* when customers discuss small quantity of goods offered for a price. He wears a rat-eaten cap soaked in oil, a worn-out cloth hanging from the bulky bust and a piece which scantily reaches down the thigh and slackens on the bulkier waist. He beats his daughter come to ask for the daily expenses of his own family with a hungry female cat bound (at his side) crying. The creditor becomes more hypocritical in Rajat (VIII 129 f.).[68] though same in appearance. In the court he wears a gentle look with an oily face (Vs. 129). With sandal marks all over his body the pot-bellied merchant resembled a scorpion and gourd (Vs. 132-3). Though fiercer than a tiger, gently he devours a deposit (Vs. 129). He spoke to the depositor in friendly protestation with smiles of expanded lips and closing eyes (Vs. 146). A merchant who embezzled a deposit shows himself alway eager to listen to sacred texts and like some other hackneyed elements in society delight in seditious tales and king's misfortunes (Rajat. III 706-10). The portraiture of the Kashmirian usurer though tinged with detestation seems to have been largely true of those in the other parts of the country then and in the present days even.

The detestation was engendered by the hard lot of the indebted. Indebtedness pervaded all sections of people, the house-holders and cultivators being worst affected. Pra. Chin[69] contains a story which refers to the harassment of a poor Brahmin by creditors and only a king's munificence could release him from their clutches. It is not likely that a poor debtor could incur a large sum, but even a *small sum might assume* dreadful proportions. A verse in uktivyakti advises

67. Karika 29, p. 42.

68. M. Gopal, *Mauryan Pub. Fin.* contemplates a commission received by the king on mortgage performed in the gambling house from Kaut. III 20, though the text is not clear on the point.

69. VIII 53 f.

repayment in full without keeping a slightest remnant.[70] A composition of Hemachandra in Jalhana's collection utters a proverbial commentary on the fate of a poor man and places debt first among the five ills attending debt, misfortune, laziness, hunger and large progeny (according to our restoration).[71] The documents show heavy pressure on the debtors in recovery. The debtor had to carry a debt in kind to creditor's granary in his own carts or by carriers (L.P. 21, L.Pr. 15) after paying king's dues and to bear the costs if any incurred by the creditor from maintenance of a pledge to recovery. *He also had to entertain with meals those who came to receive payments as known from epigraphy.* In L.P. there was no compensation provided, if a pledged animal died at creditor's fault.

Even kings were not free from the ills of indebtedness. Marco Polo (II 343) reports that a king owed a sum to a foreign merchant which he could recover by drawing a line around him on street. Sukar recommends that the king after giving a promise of paying a certain interest should take the wealth of the rich in times of crisis as a loan and when the danger passes away he should return the same with interest (IV 2. 21-22). Kalhana regrets that 'in this land..., the kings now maintained themselves by giving bills of exchange to the tantrins.[72] During the famine of 917-8 A.D. following a flood, grain sold at a fabulous price (V. 270-1) and the ministers and Tantrins became wealthy (V. 274). The king would take that person as the minister who raised the sums due on the Tantrins' bills, by selling the subjects in such a condition, yet the sums fell short.[73] As he failed to pay the Tantrins (adattahundikadeyah), the king fled in fear (V. 302). Sambhuvardhana negotiated with the Tantrin promising greater sums. Sons of ministers engaged in deep-laid plots.[74] Bankers acted as kingmakers perhaps more often than known down to modern

70. *Jat* IV 184.

71. Ibid.

72. Ibid.

73. G.O.S. no. 82.

74. Tantripam hundikadanat bhubhujum jivikabhavat. Rajat V. 266.

times. It has been suggested that Kumarapala of Gujerat received the assistance of Jain merchants in his rise to power.

Puratana prabandha samgraha relates a story of kingVisaladeva who received an amount of money or cereal (chanaka)from the banker Jagadu during a famine and relief was distributed.[75] The commentary throws light on the above text and says that the banker Jagadu gave mudhas 8000 to Visaladeva, 16000 to Hammira and 21000 to Sultan in bad times and acquired fame for the charity house thus opened in a famine.[76] These probably were loans and mudha here was a measure of capacity rather than a coin-name.[77] The amounts show that the foreign ruler enjoyed the highest credit and next to him Hammira. It is to note that the fame of the banker and not the king spread for his fulness in crisis.

Vallalasena is said to have incurred debts for political reasons in Vallalacharita composed by Gopalabhatta.[78] This story in the Uttarakhanda goes that once Vallala borrowed a crore of niskas from Vallabhananda Adaya, the richest Sauvarnika banker, for the purpose of conquering the king of Udantapura; repeatedly defeated, he wanted to make a grand bid and demanded a fresh loan of one and a half crore. Vallabhananda agreed to pay if only the revenues of Harikeli were assigned to him in payment of the debt. This enraged the king who took possession of the wealth of a large number of Vaniks (Ch. II). The tension with the money-lending class spread on the socio-political level and strained socio-economic cohesion.[79] It was reported that Vallabha was in league with the palas of Magadha, his relatives. Vallala then recast the social strata in a way to degrade the Sauvarnikas as Sudras, and upgrade the Kaivartas the old enemies of the palas. The down-grading became a legacy for later times.

75. Adheyah—prajah/vikriya vahayam nasit tantrinam hundika-dhanam/ V. 275.
76. Droha chakrikah, V. 268; compare, chakrika bhanjana, an epithet of Amoghavarsa in Ganitasara of Mahavira.
77. Ibid.
78. Ibid.
79. Cf. mutaka in Arthuna Ins. In scarcity, supply of cereal (chanaka) was more appropriate.

The number of endowment records become increasingly higher from the 10th cent. and there was a spurt in such banking. In the north endowment of hard cash or gold was rare, as there was every chance of the temple's being plundered by invaders, and there was naturally an emphasis on assignment of land, buildings, taxes and levies which a plunderer could not take away. It has already been observed that religious centres had economic functions with a secular element in the management.

The gifts of kings and officials came largely from the booty[80] in livestock and gold; the resources were distributed over the country through endowments to temples which lent these out to appropriate persons. A good amount came from merchants and devotees. Much was spent on development programme e.g. by irrigation from village tanks. This meant balancing of the social and political economy by the interpenetration of the politico-military, religious and economic spheres that has been described as a temple-assembly and temple-guild "symbiosis".[81] Besides holding land and supporting a copious staff, the temples engaged in lending their stock and trading in consecrated food (even in illicit manner) but seldom in manufacture or trading in manufactured goods, which was because most of the necessities were to be supplied as interest or could be procured with interest money, if also or other reasons suggested in the concluding chapter. The economic activity of the temple was restricted to productive pursuits indirectly through lending. We find nagaratta transferring a deposit originally made with them to temple during a change-over in its administration (no. 201, S.I.I. XIII). The weavers (pattasali) of Kanchipuram placed in the management of temple are seen in the Mad. Mus Pls of Uttama Chola. This handicapped the industrial and commercial community with new liabilities that impaired their mobility. They had to look after land and other assets of the temple. Sometimes merchants, dancing girls, drummers etc.

80. Ed. Harishchandra Kariratna; cf. R.C. Majumdar, *Hist. of Beng.* I, p. 240.

81. N.R. Ray, Vangalir Itihasa, Adiparva, p. 525.

came to possess land in this period much more than before thus adding a new dimension to the ownership of land and perhaps meaning an extra load upon land. Another implication of endowment was that these might be invested on a sectarian basis and even as a means of conversion. A large portion of the property of a Saiva temple was utilised for the benefit of Saivites, who subsequently would become converts for the sake of economic benefits.[82] Endowments to Yaksini might have a similar purpose of popularising Jain faith by attracting devotees of the mother cult as has been suggested.[83]

No account of the endowments can be exhaustive. Those for lamps were the most numerous. The merit of dedicating lamp at particular places has been stated in Danamayukha (p. 250). The expiatory aspect explained in the previous chapter is evident in numerous inscriptions besides Kutottunga's insc. no. 64 of 1900. Accidental and even culpable homicide was met with an order for the culprit to make an endowment for burning lamp towards the merit of the deceased. Thus one or two lamps, the number depending on the intensity of the crime and circumstances, were to be burnt for the accidental killing of a girl by a woman (148 of 1906) or of a wife by husband (91 of 1906) or a person stabbed to death by a merchant for an attempt at the modesty of his concubine (77 of 1906), or for fatally wounding one (67 of 1906) or when a lady was tortured by the Udaiyan to pay tax took poison (80 of 1906). Sastri has rightly remarked that the code erred on the side of leniency.[84] Another object probably was fulfilment of some vow or escaping king's wealth. A number of king's officers seem to have vowed to put up lamps in case they escaped from being disgraced by Rajaraja for the part they played in the battle of Urayur.[85] Burning for durations shorter than a day was indicated by fractional number of lamps, e.g. 1/2, 1/4 or 1½ (N.A. no. 469, 479,

82. Sastri, Hist. S. Ind, 312; B. Stein, J.A.S. Vol. 19, p 164.
83. Spencer, I.E.S.H R., 1968, p. 293, ib. 1970, p. 434, also refers to M. Nash who describes this as a 'levelling mechanism'.
84. A.V. Krishnamurty, J.A.H.R.S. Vol. 26, p. 163.
85. Cf. N.G. Unithan, J.I.H. 1966, p. 541.

517 in V.R.I). Lampstands were sometimes shaped like the donor and called danmaparipalam. Chhayadipa in Puri Pls meant lamp held in the hand of an image generally of the donor.[86] Endowment for lamp was appropriate in the form of cattle to provide ghee for burning. Generally 90 or 96 sheep were required for a lamp of full day's burning. A group of shepherds (idaiyar) were to supply 1 urakku of ghee from the assignment of 96 ewes or 48 cows or 16 she-buffaloes (no. 63, S.I.I. II) or some combination thereof (no. 94) the parity being given in the records (ibid p. 43) sometimes a part of required number being given in equivalent sum as price (no. 64). The money donated was to be converted to livestock, ewes being preferred. Buffaloes and even cows evidently were bartered for ewes, probably in consideration of low maintenance cost or extra benefits (e.g. wool?), at the rate of 1 she-buffalo=3 cows=ewes based on respective milk yield. Another consideration might be the lower amount of tax payable on each sheep. A Hoysala record that 10 Kasus were to be paid on each sheep, 30 Kasus on each cow and 100 Kasus on each buffalo, the cattle of a particular temple being exempted. Going by the barter rate given in the Chola record one would certainly prefer to exchange a buffalo for 6 ewes or a cow for 2 ewes as then he would have to pay 60 Kasu instead of 100 in the first case and 20 instead of 30 in the second. This tax rate and the exchange rate might not be prevailing everywhere, but this no doubt gives some indication. If all the temple cattle were thus exempted, then this lower tax would not be a point of preference for ewe. But then if everywhere temple cattle were exempt from taxation we get a clue to the tremendous craze for dedicating cattle to temples. Even the motive of a petty shepherd was not wholly religious in earmarking his sheep for a lamp in temple evidently keeping them with himself for the supply of the material. There would be the least trouble for the supply or its break he himself being the donor and the supplier. Sometimes the endowed sheep were described as undying and unaging (E.I. VII 196,

86. Cholas, p. 477; also I.H.Q. Sept.-Dec. 1958.

S.I.I. II no. 196). Hultzsch suggests that those sheep which died or ceased to give milk had to be replaced from among the lamps that had meanwhile grown up without hampering the supply of interest material.

Cases of gold endowed for lamp were many. Two of 30 kalanju each were made by the daughter of Parantaka I. In the same reign a merchant's wife dedicated 30 Kasu (246 of 1923-4). The headman of a village donated money for burning three lamps (51 of 1928). Rajaraja's sister donated certain sums of which two were deposited for purchasing sheep for burning lamp with ghee therefrom (S.I.I. II no. 6). Lands for lamp e.g. in Melpadi Insc. of Krsna III presumably assigned to some cattle-rearer directly or through assembly for the interest amount introduced now personnel in land utilisation.

Land and money were donated for other purposes too. Land was donated to meet expenses of angabhoga and rangabhaga in Yadava record.[87] Land for rice offerings was quite appropriate. In the 13th yr. of Rajaraja I 550 kuli of land was donated to render 4 mali of price to the deity (S.I.I. III no. 2). Land came from merchants to meet expenses of a festival (thiuvidi—91 of 1931-2) in the 38th yr. of Kulottunga. A cash of 234 Kasu was given as capital funds for renovation specially (pudukkuppuram, 571 of 1904) in Rajaraja's reign (992 A.D.). The assembly was to feed ascetics in return for 400 Kuli of tax-free land and to feed Vedic literature from land given by merchant (469, 470 of 1925-6).

On secular purposes also donations were made to be used as capital. In a record of Sundara Choa Parantaka II, the annual interest 3 Kasu on 20 Karun Kasu was to be given as prize to the best reciter of hymn in competition (no. 250, S.I.I. XIII). In a record of Rastrakuta Akalavarsa (984 A.D.) 30 matters of land, flower garden and oil-mill were set apart for the upkeep of a student's home (no. 67, S.I.I. IX). Lands given for imparting education are well on record.[88] The village tank occupied a place of vital importance in rural economy. Even a temple land was sacrificed for its construction giving

87. Hultzsch on no. 95 of S.I.I. II, p. 459.
88. S.I.I. V No. 1205 for Chhatas; D.C. Sircar, E.I. 33, p. 183.

another land to the temple in exchange (110 of 1911) under Kulottunga I. Under the Hoysalas, 200 gadyanas were granted from the interest of which at the rate of 1 bele (i.e. 15%) 30 gadyanas was to be spent for the maintenance of a village tank and its channels.[89] Land was also endowed for plying of boats in the tank (342 of 1903) etc.

According to an estimate[90] the amounts donated by Rajaraja I to the temple of Tanjore made 41,500 kalanju of gold. Parantaka I (910 A.D.) gave 60 Kal. of pure gold to fetch 60 kalam of paddy per yr. at the rate of 30 kalam at each harvest (S.I.I. III, p. 229). In the Mad. Mus Pls. of Uttam Chola, two assemblies received 250 Kal. on the undertaking to measure 500 kadi of paddy every yr. (ib. p. 273). An endowment in Chinese gold in 1019 A.D. is interesting. $87^3/_4$ kal. of Chinakkanakam for worship of Ardhanarigal in Nagapttinam, an equal amount for feeding and 60 kal. of Undigaippon were donated by the agent of kidarattaraiyar. Chinese coins found its way into Tamilnad through trade with kataha.[91] A merchant from Malainadu gave $16^1/_8$ kal. of gold in a Vadakkadan in Chingleput as a perpetual loan to feed Brahmanas from the interest (54 of 1893). Higher incidence of land endowments, which provided a place for the investment of the monetary endowment,[92] shows the assembly in more actual need of gold and cash. Cases of land sold to temples or to individuals for the temple in return for gold were many. While taxes were remitted on these in lieu of interest on the amounts received, the whole produce was diverted in compensation for the principal.

Cash endowments were not always converted into livestock but distributed in cash. Interest was to be paid either in grain or in other commodities of specific utility or in money to buy some other articles not manufactured by the assignee. These have been treated separately under the rates of interest below.

89. J.B.B.R.A.S. XII, p. 32; O.P. Verma, Yadavas etc. also Mera Visnu T. Ins , J.B.R.S.V. 52, p. 62 f.
90. S.I.I. IX nos. 133, 204, XI nos. 39, 41, 47 etc.
91. C.S. Sastri, J. of Mysore University, July, 1928, 201.
92. Sastri, Hist. S. Ind., 312.

The assignment of taxes and dues to a temple or their remission for benefit of a temple against a sum received was a perpetual endowment, the taxes representing the interest. When self-imposed taxes or levies were paid by a guild or a community for no sum reeeived, these perpetually paid donations went to add to the loanable assets of a temple. The donations of tax-income (teru) from five mudas of land granted for offerings in the Dharesvara Ins. (1083 A.D.)[93] or of those on land in Mudanir for services etc. of a temple was probably a fiscal transfer. In a record from Bijapur (1092 A.D.) 500 merchants made over an impost due to them (I.A. VI 138). The Arthuna Ins. (1080 A.D. E.I. XIV 295 f) enlists dues from sales in the market assigned to temple by Yasodeva and others : 1 dra. on each house and shop of braziers, 1 rupak on Bengal madder, 2 on a gambling house, 4 on a vumvaka of distillers, levies on certain commodities and so on. The Rajor Ins. (960 A.D. E.I. III 263 f) mentions taxes assigned on a gift village in Raputana; 2 Vimsopakas on every sack of agricultural produce brought to the market (hattavyavaharika), 2 on each vithi and levies on ghee, oil etc. In an insc. of 953 A.D. the Guhila king Allata of Ahar assigns 1 dramma on the sale of an elephant, 2 rupakas on a horse, levies on oil millers, garlanders and so on (I.A. Vol. 58, p. 161). The next king gave 14 dra. to the sun temple yearly.[94] The Bayana Ins. of Chitralekha (955 A.D.—E.I. XXII 120) records donations to Visnu; 3 dra. daily collected at mandapika (custom house) of Sripatha, 3 at vusavata, 1 on a horse sold or a horse-load of merchandise. The Somanatha T. Ins. also records donations out of the mandapika tax. The Harsa St. Ins. (970 A.D.) records endowments of 1 vimsopaka on every Kutaka of salt, 1 dra. on a horse sold.[95] The Bali St. Ins. (1103 A.D.) records grant of 4 dra. towards festival of goddess Vahugrna, 1 dra.

93. Krishna, J.N.S.I., XX 13. Chinese coins have been discovered from Tanjore dist. Trade contact of Karnataka with S.E. Asia is confirmed by Javanese sources, E.I. III 297.

94. Capital was invested in land, Trav. Arch. Ser. III 43.

95. E.I. Vol. 38 No. 14.

on every horse sold during horse-fair and so on.[96] The Nadlai Ins. (1138 A.D.—E.I. XI 36) records grant of 1/20 part of abhavya (income) derived from the loads of bullocks ingress towards lamp etc. The Partabgarh Ins. of Mahendrapala III (946 A.D., E.I. XIV 176) consolidates the previous grants to deities in the shrine of Vatayaksini—one palika of oil per mill (ghana) and other measures on saffron, betelnuts etc. (Vanigvarggena). In Sanderav Ins. queen grants 1 dra. from revenue and an impost from cart-makers. Twelve families of fishermen were to pay 3/4 kal. per head on their earnings towards a festival by Rajaraja I (274 of 1910). In a Dharwar Insc. (1080 A.D.) certain guilds agree to pay a measure of paddy collected from different shops (K.I. i 14-23). In a Yadava insc. from Managali (1161 A.D.), guilds of svamis, sethis, gavaras, nakharas, oilmen, artisans, toddy-drawers, mat-makers etc. gave levies and taxes in visa on rubies, grain, cotton, oil etc. towards lamp festival including a marriage-tax (also in 167 of 1910). Gadyanas were donated for supply of flowers.[97] Such benefactions known as magamai were frequently made (S.I.I. III no. 78 etc.). Chalikya Vikramaditya VI assigned a share in the proceeds of fines levied in Puli to Siva (E.I. V. 18, p. 189). In certain records, oil mills, house-sites, flower gardens and imposts were donated.[98] Rajadhiraja I assigned tax on oil mill (sekkirai), viniyoga, loomsmiths etc. towards festivals (no. 195 in V.R.I. p. 345). Houses were donated in the Bhatera Ins. (1949 A.D.—E.I. XIX 277) and the Mathura Pr. (1050 A.D.). In the latter two houses and six shops were given among other things by Jajja who possibly represented both the varga (guild) and the gosthi (temple authorities).[99] The Siyodoni Ins. which is a collection of records (903-969 A.D.) states the endowments mostly by private persons of avasanika (residence), vithis (shops) and certain imposts. They were Nagaka, Bhaila

96. J. Orient Res. V. 29, p. 96; Udaipura Rajyaka Ithihasa, p. 130.

97. I.A. Vol. 42, p. 60.

98. E.I. IX 32.

99. Prachina Marathi Lekha no. 34.

and others including betel-seller (pp. 11-18, 21-27, 31-36). In Sam 1025 Sridhara assigned 1/4 adivaraha dra. paid as rent of a vithi (p. 36-9). Merchant Nagaka gave capital of 1350 Srimadadivaraka dra. invested with distillers (in Sam 969) who were to pay 1/2 Vigraphatungiya dra. monthly on every cask of liquor to Visnu (pp. 28-30). Distillers were to give liquor to Visnu worth 1/2 vigrahapala dra. on another endowment (Sam 965, tali datavya, 8-10). If there was no mistake in presentation in these lines one has to contemplate the use of liquor in the temple of Visnu. The Mahajanas of Dosihatta gave a monthly assignment of 1/3 dra. to Bhailasvami (pp. 28-9) and 2 Karsa on certain Yugas (pp. 20-1). Stone-cutters assigned 1/3 Vigra. dra. and oil millers a paloka of oil per mill (pp. 29-31). We thus find that while tax and levy on oil had a very high incidence, the trend to endow vithi and house or its rent was greater than before. Unlike the Ahar or Kaman Ins. the Siyodomi does not state that the donations of house by merchants were in consideration of any sums received from the temple. This may signify that the merchants in the 10th cent. were better off.

6

Donors–Donees–Land Mortgage by Temples

(FROM 900-1200 A.D.)

Donors

Endowment of grain in individual capacity was made by two merchants in Karnataka (K.I.i. 14-23). A chief granted an allowance of paddy to a deity installed by a dancing girl (11 of 1903). The installation of a temple by dancing girl (devaradiyar) and the fact that they figure prominently as donors in the endowment picture testify to their social rise coupled with economic strength. The giver of 90 sheep for lamp (147 of 1912), Chaturan Chaturi was the wife of Nagan. The profession by then did not bar married life. That they were in possession of land is proved by donations to the temples (345 of 1911, 153 of 1906) etc. In the reign of Visnuvardhana (1141 A.D.) another gifted 50 inupa yedli for lamp. Many such donations in cash or gold have been recorded (36 of 1895, no. 1079, V.R. p. 1371 etc.). Donations by concubines occur alongside those by queens in a religious shrine. Rekamadevi the concubine of Permadi gave 6 uttamaganda madas. Donors comprised the queen, chief, general, nobles and assembly men, guild chief, priest, accountants etc. (e.g. S.I.I. II no. 82).

Spencer[1] tabulates and quantifies certain endowments to the Tanjore temple. From his table (p. 287) it appears that

1. I.E.S.H.R. 1968, pp. 283, 285.

out of 9097 Kasu donated in all, king's contribution was 360, that of military officers was 7211 and from others came 1526, most of the money coming from the money and 84% of livestock and that the motives were mixed—religious merit, status aspiration and political submission (pp. 284-5). One should remember however that the inscriptions studied are of Spencer's own selection, which lessens the statistical value of the estimate. In a study of the endowment records in Tirupati leaning on the 16th cent. (1509-68 A.D.) B. Stein[2] observes that donations largely came from state personages and next to them from temple functionaries (p. 165). One of the donors (no. 95, S.I.I. II) was Jonaka Savur Paranjodi, a foreigner. The editor suggests (p. 328) that he might be a Greek in the background of Indo-Roman trade. Another foreign donor was an Arab (Tajika) feudatory of Indra III and a viceroy of Sanjan in an insc. from Thana dist.[3] Grants by merchants increased in this period and they enjoyed a large measure of autonomy in levying cesses and taxes irrespective of state authority.[4] They derived this power as a highly organised and broad-based community. Viravananju merchants made benefaction to Jain and Saiva temples alike to suit the religious propensities of their clients and compatriots. Ubhaya-Nanadesis operating in and outside India made perpetual donations to Buddhist monastery and a Tara temple in a like manner.[5] Sometimes guilds of various descriptions (e.g. Nanadesis, Gatrigas, Svamis, Nakharas) assembled to take a collective decision for making grants.[6] While there is no evidence to prove that they granted land oftener than money or gold[7] in many cases they made grants of land by purchase,[8] which indicates that they did not grant

2. J.A S. XIX 163 f.
3. Cf. Sircar, Stud. in Rel. Life, p. 125.
4. B.N. Puri, Hist. of Gurjara-Pratiharas, p. 131.
5. I.A X 185; S.I.I. IX 297.
6. E I V. 23; K.I. I, 39-40; Appadorai, I, 387; Gururajachar, Asp. Ec. Soc. Life etc., p. 117.
7. Cf. D.N. Jha, Sarkar Fel. Vol. p. 118; 274 of 1923, 449 of 1925; of 1926 etc.
8. S.I.I. III No. 100, 121 of 1929-30, 17 of 1939-40 etc.

land possessed by them in all cases or perhaps that they did not possess much of it. As a contrast, ordinary donors of lands in certain cases held the right to cultivate them (Karanmai), paying to the temples a tax in grain at a fixed rate (409 of 1914). Under the Kaniyatchi system, tenancy was retained by the donor by paying a yearly sum or a share in the yield.[9]

The Mulgund Ins. of Krsna II records endowment jointly by donors, a field by 4 guild-chiefs and another by some Brahmins to a temple of Jina. This is interesting also for the religious attitude [10] A joint gift by two chiefs comprised 2 visa per mada of salt out of the sale-proceeds. All the endowments by guilds were of joint nature. As seen in Managali Ins. artisans, oilmen, basket-makers, betel leaf sellers, toddy-drawers etc. and stone-cutters in Siyodoni Ins. were organised in some form or other to become joint donors (also S.I.I. II no. 82). The payment by rathakaras in Sanderav Ins. was probably made at royal order, as it occurs along with a queen's dedication of land revenue. Agriculturists combined to give annually one padakku of paddy for each plough and one kuruni for each man to a temple (117 of 1900). Donations in individual capacities are instanced by a shepherd (60 sheep, S.I.I. XIII no. 209), a weaver (130 Kasu, 292 of 1902) and a door-keeper (3 perpetual donations to be continued by his descendants—I.A. XI 337). A hunter (vettuvar) could donate a land for 3 Kal. (S.I.I. III no. 24) and a drummer could offer gold for lamp (27 of 1895). A musician deposited 40 Kasu, the interest on which was to be paid to 5 drummers on festival days. An artist gifted 30 gadyanas in 1079 A.D. (Bk no. 43, A.R.E. 1933-4). The donor composition shows the rise of the artisan class at the social scale with merchants and nobles at the top.

Donees

A Buddhist monastery[11] received 820 patakas of land from Srichandra in Bengal. A Jain monastery got villages from

9. Stein, ib. p. 166.
10. E.I. vol. 27, p. 10—gadyanas for flower by persons.
11. Sircar, Stud. Rel. Life, p. 196, does not think that matha always meant monastery.

Indra III, the donee being names as Vardhamana (E.I. V. 38, 9.5). On behalf of another Jain monastery the priest Kanakasena received the donation (E.I. V. 13, p. 190). Thus in the case of mathas the lands granted were considered to be the property of the head of the matha; where the donee was a temple, the land was held in trust with idol as the juristic person.[12] Yaksa worship shared the popularity of Jain faith, and a queen's servant offered lamp to Yaksa (65 of 1903). Vatayaksini (Partabgarh Ins.) was an aspect of Durga by adoption, which was related to the spread of the mother cult. Saptamatrkas received land (705 of 1909) and taxes were exempted on land for their worship and the priests were called Matrsivas (no. 191, S.I.I. III).

It was obligatory on the part of the bodies or persons with whom an endowment was invested to give two meals a day to the man sent to collect the interest which was made a condition in L.P. (21) and some inscriptions.[13] The practice continued to modern times. An insc. adds that the credentials of such persons were to be verified (E.I. VII 143). Grains paid as interest were to be clean and delivered in the temple-yard at borrower's cost (E.C. IX Cp. 129).

Village assemblies were the chief recipients in investment, especially when the supplies were in rural products. Sometimes separate deposits had been jointly invested with an assembly as recorded in the Mad. Mus. Pls.

Villagers were to measure 150 Kalam of paddy upon 600 Kasu, the total of two deposits, 94 and 506 (S.I.I. II no. 19). In one instance a loan was jointly incurred by merchants (nagarattar) and villagers (140 of 1912). For the supply of ghee group responsibility was preferred. Probably there was risk in relying on a particular body of shepherds. The risk was distributed by assignment with several groups of shepherds, their names and addresses being particularly recorded (no. 95, S.I.I. II). The hinterland of the Tanjore temple might be wider than the network of cattle assignment would

12. A.C. Ghosh, Law of Endow, p. 8f.
13. 512 of 1911, E.I. V. 26, p. 230.

suggest.[14] The addresses indicate that shepherds living in or near Tanjore received the major share. The cattle were not to be returned.

Investment with trade guilds is seen in many records as they formed an important organ of self-government.[15] It is said that there are few instances in the north of guilds accepting endowments and paying periodical interest on account of troubled conditions and that frequent migrations did not leave the guilds stable.[16] No split-up of guild has been recorded in this period. Guildhood accompanied the growth in commercial activity, and oil-mongers, stone-cutters and even distillers were sufficiently organised to bind themselves to perpetual payments. The seller of betel leaves had good economic stability to endow house and shop. Distillers were of sufficient credit to receive investment of a large sum from a merchant. The impost they paid was but perpetual interest on the sum. It appears that the distillers in 810 also received a sum from a merchant which he acquired from potters. As Nagaka gave a palika of oil on every mill, it appears that he loaned an amount to the oil-millers. It is possible that the tithes to be paid by artisans and producers as per instructions of the merchants were in lieu of interest on some advances received from them or the temple. There had been fewer endowments in gold or cash for the N. Indian temples, because they were open to frequent plunder. They received endowments of lands, houses and tithes not to be carried away. In 1043 A.D. a money deposit was lent to nagarattar or mercantile town committee (140 of 1912). In no. 37 of S.I.I. II, 360 Kasu were lent to four bazars @ 1/8 Kasu per Kasu per yr. to provide plantains from the total interest of 45 Kasu.

The citizens of Mummudi Sora high street (perunderu) and Virasikhamani high street received 120 Kasu each, and the citizens of Nittavinoda high street and Tribhubanamahadevi great market (perangadi) received 60 Kasu each. Of the two deposits made by Gunapati in the 29th yr. of Rajaraja I (no.

14. Spencer, I. E.S.H.R. 1968, p. 281.
15. Moraes, Kadambakula, p. 285.
16. L. Gopal, Op. cit., 175.

24, ib.), 56 Kasu were lent to the inhabitants of the Tribhubanamahadevi market near Tanjavur to procure from the interest-sum big champaka buds and cardamon seeds. The other sum of 30 Kasu was invested with villagers to provide khas khas roots. The distribution in this inscription is not typical of the entire collection of money-lending records, for here the merchants received a sum that was nearly double of that lent to villagers, while in the general picture the assemblies figures as the most prominent recipient. The specific reason here was that the investment with merchants was for things not easily procurable. The credit of the Tribhubanamahadevi market was high as it received the higher amount in nos. 24 and 37, ib. In nos. 6 and 11, investment was made with several bodies. In no. 6 king's sister deposited certain sums subsequently borrowed by separate village bodies in parts at 12½% interest per yr. Some of them were to pay interest in grain, others in money and individuals in ghee towards the deity's requirements including cloth. Two individuals received 64 Kasu (=32+32) to buy sheep. Besides there were 9 village bodies receiving 10 sums. No assembly received sums twice except Parantaka Chaturvedi Mangalam which got 600 Kasu (112+488) out of 3000 Kasu i.e. 20% of the total investment, sums of investment ranging from 100 to 520 Kasu. No merchant community occurs in the list. Speaking in general a bulk of the donor's contribution was invested with the assemblies.[17] In a study of certain Tanjore records, Spencer has observed that of 9097 Kasu donated village assemblies borrowed 8681 or 95.4% and the merchants 416 i.e. 4.6% (ib. p. 287, Table IV). This reflects an emphasis on rural development as also the high or low credit needs of villagers and merchants respectively.

In an insc. ascribed to Rajadhiraja II, the temple invested a sum with a religious community, the Siva-Brahmanas who agreed to burn a lamp for the interest. As some of them fled in the wake of some trouble (connected by the editor with the Pandyan succession war), others met to disburse the unpaid

17. Ibid.

dues on their deserted lands which they sold to the temple. Investment with individuals is also known. In a record of Sundara Chola 124 veli of temple land was assigned to a person on permanent tenancy lease on condition that he should supply 120 kalam of paddy per veli (no. 236, S.I.I. (XIII). Another record speaks of a lease of land to a merchant by the priests of a temple (46 of 1913) Land and house were leased by a temple to a headman for the supply of pepper (266 of 1911). The lessees became powerful landed interests as the Nayakas were in the Vijayanagara empire.[18] There is a pious wish in a Chola insc. that even if the property changes hands by sale or mortgage, the endowment duty was to be performed by the alienee (637 of 1909). Even female descendants were enjoined to continue the feeding for gift entrusted in the absence of male ones (S.I.I. III no. 210). It means that the capital was not to be returned. The Puri Ins. of Chodaganga[19] records a case in which it was probably returned and the investee was changed. Three priests had donated gold (1.6) for chhayadipa or lamp held in the hand of an image of the donor to Markandesvara. On the termination of the old endowment the donors created a fresh one by depositing the same gold with another person Jivanta Sresthin (a merchant) for the supply of 200 measures of oil. According to Dr. Sircar, the editor, 1.4 suggests that Bhimadeva's son Nana arranged for the discharge of the obligation; probably after Bhimadeva's death Nana refunded the deposit and freed himself from the obligation. This might be an occasion for the revision of interest rate. Where the safety of a principal was in question it had to be produced by the borrowers every five years before the temple committee (1195 A.D.—264 of 1913). This may be compared with M. VIII 155—adarsayitva hiranyam. In a Chola insc. drummers (uvachchars) were considered of sufficient credit as the assignee of an endowment to the temple. Similarly, a dancing woman and her descendants were entrusted with a village by assembly for performances to be held before a deity (370 of 1909).

18. N. Karashima, J.E.S.H.O., May, 1976, p. 227.
19. E.I. V. 33, p. 183.

Three modes of interest payment operated in money (cash or gold), in grain and in specified commodities other than grain.[20] In the last case nothing but the specified articles of consumption, e.g. oil,[21] ghee, were to be accepted as interest. In one instance, interest was invariably to be in kind and not in coin, any irregularity being punishable.[22] For interest in paddy a particular variety was stated, e.g. Kuttai paddy, white paddy of spring variety or black paddy of summer (E.C. IX) Cp. 129). The grain interest was to be paid in the time of harvest (S.I.I. II no. 54). In one instance monetary interest was to be paid every six months (S.I.I. III no. 105). Sometimes in the same endowment interest was to be paid on one sum in money and on another in grain (nos. 6, 9, 26, S.I.I. II). With the paddy interest on the second deposit (78 Kasu) in no. 26 other requirements were to be procured (by barter) but the first deposit (16 Kasu) was to provide for camphor which had to be bought, whence the insistence on interest in coin (2 Kasu). This perhaps indicates that certain articles e.g. camphor could not be easily procured in barter. Though inscriptions rarely record an option to pay either in money or kind (60 kal. or 225 Kadi of paddy, 282 of 1906), this possibly was allowed in practice in want of money or particular commodities in certain cases. The incidence of grain interest was considerably higher than that of monetary interest as it appears from certain epigraphs recording both individually. In no. 6 (ib), out of the total sum 3000 Kasu, 2040 were lent on grain interest, 896 on monetary interest and 64 for interest in ghee. In no. 9, 1070 were put on grain interest and 180 on cash interest with the same villagers, and in no, 26, 78 were on grain interest and 16 on cash interest.

Rates have differed according as the interest was in money or kind and as the capital was in gold or grain. The widely divergent rates of interest in kind and money may be observed separately before they are compared. Although particular

20. Ibid.
21. S.I.I. XIII.
22. 263 of 1910; A.R.E. 1911—II para 19.

rates are fixed in the inscriptions once for all, the rates of interest in actual payment in kind might have fluctuated with the rise or fall in prices of an interest commodity, where prices are known, the rate p.c. can be worked out approximately, but there is no much divergence in measure and exchange value that it will be absolutely unsafe to reach a conclusion.

The rate is evident where grain is paid as interest on grain. Normally grain was paid by a special measure for interest, which was a kalam of 90 nali (=15 kuruni of 6 nali each). In special cases, kalam of 96 nali (=12 kuruni of 8 nali each), the ordinary measure was specified in paying interest. In one instance, 56 Kadi of paddy by the 8 nali measures was stated as the interest on 15 kal. of gold (S.I.I. III no. 186). The same measure was followed in 512 of 1911. Grain as interest on gold was stipulated in many other documents. 92 Kadi of paddy on 92 kal. of gold (no. 190, ib) and 90 Kadi on 20 kal. (22 of 1888) indicate wide divergence. If the price 60 kal. for 225 Kadi of paddy quoted in N. Arcot in Rajaraja's 12th yr. (282 of 1906) can be taken as prevailing in Conjeeveram in the same year of his reign, then 140 kadi as interest on 33 kal. of gold (18 of 1888) would give the rate of interest as 115%. Even if this rate be not approximate, it is significantly indicative of the high rate of interest in grain carried by a gold loan. In a record in the reign of Krsna III from S. Arcot, 20 kal. of gold placed by a Vaidumba queen carried 20 kalam of paddy as interest.[23] As price of paddy varied then from 8 to 10 kalam per kal., Altekar (ib. p. 373) works out the rate as 8-12½%. He arrives at 10-15% on another loan (E.I. VII 188), where 1 kalam for 1 kal. was by the perumalai measure (25% bigger). In the 29th yr. of Rajendra I merchants (nagarattar) and villagers (140 of 1912) jointly agreed to pay 90 kalam of paddy as interest on a sum 2 kalam per kal. The grain rate on gold went up to 3 kalam per kal. (58 of 1897) and 4 kalam (90 of 1928). The same temple at the same time received different rates of interest, 2/3 kalam and 1 kalam per kal. per yr. (Mad. Mus. Pls. 28-34). In Rajendra's 6th yr. a

23. S.A. No. 636, V.R I. (referred as N.A. 636 in Altekar, pp. 373, 378 f.n. 96).

lower rate is shown by 64 kalam for 150 kasu (91 of 1892). The rate appears as considerably lower in some records of Rajaraja and Rajendra (nos. 6, 9, 10, 26—S.I.I. II etc.), where money was put on grain interest 3 kuruni per yr. Kasu. If the Kasu was not much devalued or if its exchange value was the same by a remote possibility, the rate would be much lower than that in the Pandya inscriptions of Varaguna II, (2 kalam per Kasu). As the measure too might differ, it may not be right to describe the rate in the Chola insc. as 1/8 of that in the Pandya insc. If we surmise that the rate 8 Kasu per Kasu was applicable to the interest in grain on the same records (nos. 6, 9, 26 ib), the grain rate would also be 12½%. If the rate was not the same and if the Kasu was not drastically devalued to make paddy so dear, one has to presume that interest in grain on cash was abnormally low as a contrast to interest in grain on gold which was abnormally high. This however was not always the case; 1 kalam per Kasu has been noticed in 214 of 1911 and 2 tuni 3 kuruni in abnormal times of flood and famine (307 of 1913). We can be definite on the rate of interest in grain on capital (nellumudal). 25% is shown by 25 Kadi on 100 Kadi (no 317, S.I.I. XIII) and 30 kalam on 120 kalam (no. 209, S.I.I. III). 50% is shown by 390 kalam on 780 kalam (no. 80, ib). and 75% in 232 of 1923. 30% is called dharmapallisai in 506 of 1920. 100 kalam on 320 kalam in 512 of 1911 ($3^3/_4$ kuruni on 1 kalam) shows about $31^1/_4$% repayable at two instalments at the harvests. The divergence cannot be definitely explained.

Different rates were adopted in payment of other commodities as interest. Whereas more than 18 kal. were placed as capital for the supply of a quarter measure of oil daily in one case, only 10 kal. were placed for the same purpose (264 of 1913, 63 of 1892).

Money rates show similar divergences. In an insc. of Parantaka's reign, the rate was 15% (3 manjadi per kal.), but in another (in that of his officer) it was 40% @ 1/4 puttakam per month per ilakkasu (Ceylon kasu=7½ pattakam). 15% seen in an insc. of Krsna III (22nd yr.) from Tiruvorriyur and also in many Chola records[24] has been called the righteous rate (dharmappalisai) in 19 of 1907. 12½% occurs similarly in many records—1/8 Kasu (or 1½ akkam) per Kasu per yr. in nos. 6, 9-12, 24, 25, 26, 28 etc., S.I.I. II. It was nearly the same in no. 250 of S.I.I. XIII—3 Kasu on 20 karunkasu. Higher rates are found—25% in 57 of 1928, 518 of 1920 (10 Kasu on 40 Kasu), 50% in 193 of 1925, 281 of 1910 (@ 1/2 Kasu per Kasu). 1/8 tiramam per month per Kasu occurs in 1 of 1893. The value of Kasu was not always the same. An old Kasu apparently of finer gold and higher value fetched 1½ diramam as interest and the later debased Kasu fetched on 1/4 or 1/8 diramam (S.I.I. VIII no. 40, IV no. 813). In a majority of cases cited in Table no. XII of Pran Nath (p. 93), the rate of interest was 12½% which he thinks to have been the normal rate. In Appadorai's Table (App. V) for the period 10th-15th cent. the rates range from 8% to 90% yearly. From 909 to 1200 A.D., 12½% is seen in 17 out of 74 cases cited, occurs in the records belonging to the period from 992 to 1024 A.D.; within this period it claims a definite majority (17 out of 30 cases) and occurs only once in the 10th cent. 8% occurs only in one case of 1060 A.D., 10% in 1112 A.D., 15% in 4 cases in the whole range up to 1200 A.D., 16²/₃% in 1053 A.D., and 20% in 905 A.D. 25% appears twice in 1077 and 1098 A.D. 30-40% rates occur in 7 cases from 939 to 1194 and 30-37½% from 1014 to 1194 A.D., 30% and 37½% occurring twice each. The higher rates 45%, 75% and even perhaps 180% occur once each between 1039 and 1169 A.D. According to Appadorai, the last two were exceptional, and the usual rates varied between 12½% and 30%. As the table is selective the statistical evidence is not conclusive. According to some,[25] the temple authorities lent at low charitable rates to friends and relatives and at commercial rates to others. The high rates occur in the 12th cent. generally. It is difficult to mark out a rate as normal from this picture, though 12½% was predominant in a span of 3 decades.

24. 75 of 1893; 164, 169, 172, 179 of 1912, 176 of 1915, 216 of 1921 etc.

25. Chatterji, Op. cit., pp. 72-3.

Sastri[26] does not think that the differences were due to loan-purposes of political conditions affecting social security. The Rastrakuta invasion did not affect prevailing rate of interest as may be seen from inscriptions quoting Krsna's regnal years (179 of 1912), whereas higher and lower rates prevailed in the reign of Rajendra when there was little threat to internal security. But we should also remember that the aggressive wars of Rajendra put Chola economy at times on war footing. Appadorai rightly observes that variation in rates might give an index to the degree of security in the kingdom; the deeper effect of economic and other factors on the interest structure must also be kept in mind. Derrett[27] has shown the rates varying between 625 p.c. to 75 p.c. per yr. on the Hoysala records during 1060-1297 A,D. No one rate occurs twice on the Table. 75% that occurs in 1169 and 25% in 1172 were not much removed in time. The value of money had fallen since the Kannanur principality had been established and remained the prime cause of distress and a poor standard of public order. As a result of this, according to Derrett (pp-132-.:), the rate of interest which a depositor could obtain was remarkably lowered. On the other hand, in the context of an increasing population, oil-sellers, goldsmiths and others wanted to increase their working capital and inspired the confidence of depositors. The farm took the risk of a fall in income when they promised a high rate of interest (ib. pp. 230-1). 1160 A.D. was a year of battle, but the rates were low in a period of unrest. In 1169 during Ballala's regency, there had been outbreaks in the empire to account for the exceptional rate 75%. A.D. 1194, the year of Ballala's military operations, saw the 30% rate. Thus the periods of trouble saw both low and high rates of interest lending little consistency to the view of political turmoil as the chief factor affecting credit. The effect of economic forces was deeper in respect of the urge to borrow and the capacity to pay. Other rates are shown in a record of Bhulokamalla (.132 A.D.)—4

26. Cholas, p. 600.

27. Hoysalas, p. 231.

visas per pon on 20 gadyanas (E.I. V.37, p. 189). 25% was the interest on 6 gadyanas deposited with the merchants of Sivapura by a lady in 1077 A.D. (1 more gadyana was likewise given). In the Chahamana records, 33$^1/_3$% is shown in a Bhinmal Ins. (1206 A.D.), and 30% shown by other inscriptions (e.g. Abu Ins.) was the usual rate according to D. Sharma,[28] who thinks that the high rates were for encouraging donations, as the money market was adversely affected by the activities of the Sultans in Malwa. He explains the lower rates in the Jalor insc. (12%, 10%) of slightly later dates on the ground that the Mahabira temple there patronised by Jain merchants had little need of fresh deposits and enjoyed high credit.[29] This is cogent. Had other temples been deprived of such patronage? Thus we see that no one factor can account for such wide divergences in the interest rates. We also find that the grain rate on grain capital was seldom less than 25% and hardly more than 75%: the grain rate on gold capital rose to more than 100%. This only reflects the acute need of gold felt by the assemblies continuing from the earlier period, so that they were prepared to measure any amount as interest from grains at its disposal. On the other hand they possessed little cash to offer as interest on gold or money.

Fine for default mentioned in certain records may be noted. For a day's failure of interest, it was 8½ kanam in an insc. of Parantaka I (E.I. XXVI 230) and almost the same (8$^1/_4$ kanam) to be paid to dharmasana in the inst. of Rajakesari (262 of 1910). The interest in oil was the same in both. In default of the same daily interest in oil 4$^1/_4$ kanam was to be paid to the council of justice and 1 manjadi to the king in the 4th yr. of Parakesari (268 of 1910). 4$^1/_4$ kanam occurs also in no. 87, S.I.I. XIII and 12 kanam in no. 105 S.I.I. III. The penal interest was 1/8 pon for a day's default in the 7th yr. of Gandaraditya (168 of S.I.I. XIII and in the 3rd yr. of Rajakesari (295 of 1906), while in the 12th yr. of Rajakesari I

28. Early Chauhan Dyn. pp. 300-1.

29. Ibid., p. 301 fn. 29.

it was 1/4 pon on a yearly interest of 140 Kadi of paddy (18 of 1888). In S.I.I. III no. 186, the villagers agreed to measure the yearly interest in paddy for a year's default on some future occasion. This seems to be payment of an arrear rather than an equal amount as fine.

An insc. (E.C. IX Cp. 129) empowered the persons deputed by a temple to demand the grain interest 'to resort to if necessary to processes of distraint, such as stopping the supply of water and fire surrounding the habitation and impounding cattle'. The borrowers in this case were the members of the sabha of Vendur. Whether such sanctions were applied to extort arrears by the temple is not known, but state intervention in failure of endowment terms is well on record.

Failure and Enquiry

The opportunities for such lapses have been discussed in the previous chapter. The temple did not enjoy the full income which was interrupted by malafide tenants, or the assembly men or the accountants or the priests or a combination of them. Investigations into the affairs of the temple, especially relating to endowment lands, were characteristic of the Chola monarchs for more than the Pallavas or the Pandyas. Gross abuses created a serious concern and auditing of temple accounts was an innovation of Rajaraja I. It was no aggressive intrusion on his part that he looked into such matters mostly on royal initiative. Requests for the same presaged investigations by his successors, in which tenants complained against priests and priests against assembly. A record in the 4th yr. of Rajaraja I refers to the enquiry about the misappropriation of the lands of Agnisvara temple and the reduction of offerings (283 of 1906). Similar enquiry is mentioned in S.I.I. III p. 102. Hence the exigency of preserving copies of old endowments, especially during renovation of the shrines; copies were made of the money endowments for lamp in a temple before all the stones bearing them were used up in rebuilding the central shrine (199 of 1907). The writing on a stone recording gift of land had been erased by chiselling to render enquiry of a peculation difficult (210 of 1908). In the 26th yr. of Rajaraja

I, the auditor passed an order for the assembly that the paddy due to the temple was since to be calculated in a larger measure, thus providing for a new ritual. In the 4th yr. of Parakesari, the scale of offering was enhanced after enquiry (no. 203, S.I.I. III). It was argued by the defendants that the land was not kudinikki or freed from tenancy right. The assembly was measuring 160 kalam while the document made in the previous year showed 256 to be measured. The balance thus accumulated was converted into a capital and it was ordered that a higher scale of expenses may be adopted. Does this indicate realisation of compound interest? On a cattle endowment, the upasakas were made to pay 24 kal and 2 ma towards their unremitted quantity (299 of 1904, no 328 of S.I.I. XVII). Embezzlement by priests was punished by imposition of a fine. In 1225 A.D. (Rajaraja III) land of two accountants had been confiscated for defalcation of temple property and an amount credited to temple treasury (70-71 of 1931-2). Temple lands wrongfully sold and made tax-free was restored at king's order (no. 21, S.I.I. II).

Land Mortgage by Temple

Mortgage of temple land to an individual is found in this period also. In the 16th yr. of Rajakesari the temple authorities pledged land in Tanjore dist. to Tiruvalli Irayeri, a maid servant of the queen for 16 kal and odd. Financial necessity may be guessed from the reference in this record to 4 kal. due to the temple from some tenants (134 of 1926)—S.I.I. XIII no. 266). In modern concept the trustees have limited power of alienating temple property by mortgage etc.; this right is to be measured by necessity and may be allowed only in crisis and not for earning profit. It was in the context of illicit transfer of temple property that the villagers of Vayatur agreed that they would neither purchase nor mortgage lands belonging to temple (363 of 1908). The land mortgaged by assembly to one Mappani and redeemed by Sembiyan was endowed by the latter to temple (129 of 1914). A record ascribed to Gandaraditya or Sundara Chola palaeographically registers mortgage of a land for the dues of 2000 kal by Aiyan, a resident scholar of the village to the temple in Kurumburnadu (267 of 1925—no. 19 of S.I.I. XIII). In the Rewa Pls (1212 A.D.) of the Kalachuri period, a village Atira was mortgaged (vitta-bandhataya, 1. 19) by a Saiva teacher Santasiva. Ranaka Dharaka, the mortgagee was allowed the right to collect taxes, thus enjoying the pledge till the amount (not stated) was paid up. The editor N.P. Chakraborty notes that probably Chandella conquest was very recent and the teachers had lost the patronage of the Kalachury kings, whence the alienation of a gift village.

Land was sometimes granted with the right to sell or mortgage in the Hoysala period and when so mortgaged the alienee would be obliged to pay the revenue demand. In other cases this right was not given and temple lands were usually made tax-free. In a record in N. Arcot, the donees were required not to mortgage a gift land (30 of 1911). Not-to-be-mortgaged and not-to-be-sold occur in many inscriptions.[30] A record of Kulottunga registers sale by sabha of land which belonged to two absconding accountants towards their unpaid debts (164 of 1906). When the auditor of temple accounts detected that a person had fallen in arrears of dues, a separate land had to be assigned by him (no. 199, S.I.I. XII). Another temple came to the assistance of person in financial difficulty. When some tenants went away without paying dues on land, the Brahmin sureties being pressed for payment tried to transfer the lands to others but in vain. The temple committee met their request by buying the lands (503 of 1926). Tax evasion and absconsion for unpaid debts were frequent (S.I.I. XII p. 173). A record of Sundara Chola registers sale of land to temple by two brothers to meet fine (danda kanam of 72 kal.) imposed by assembly on their brother who was not to be found (dead or absconding). Their portions and that of a surety got mixed up in the sold land and had to be cleared at king's order on representation (no. 260, S.I.I. XIII). This shows that coparceners became liable while the surety stood by and that a co-sharer could become a surety.

30. Spencer, I.E.S.H.R. 1970, p. 441.

Temples lent to assembly for secular purposes too. An insc. (1105 A.D.) shows that a temple lent 3 pon to villagers in Pudukottai state for the purchase of a house-site, pressed them when it amounted to 7½ kal. with interest and got lands in realisation.[31] This shows crossing of doubling limit incidentally. Another refers to land made over by residents to temple for amount borrowed on the pledge of jewels (ib. no. 548). A Chola insc. refers to a loan of 60 Kasu @ 2 tuni 3 kuruni per month by temple to assembly in 'bad time' and scarcity of grain (307 of 1913). The rate may be compared to 3 kuruni per Kasu at earlier times. Temple loans to cultivators in times of need is recorded and in 1178 A.D. 50 cultivators obtained a loan of 1 gadyana each in the Haysala kingdom (E.C.IV. Velur 83). Loans to individuals to perform social obligation is also on record. A distressed father borrowed from temple treasury for daughter's marriage on personal credit (E.C. VI Mud 62). When again the arrears of taxes on a land devolved upon the sons and widow of a deceased landholder and no surety was found to stand for them, they could pay only a portion by raising loans from the treasury of two temples and from the Malaiyalar and left the village. The assembly was then empowered to realise the balance by selling their lands and house-sites to one of the temples. We get here an indication that a money-lending group from Malaimandalam in the west coast had established a settlement in the Tamil land by the middle of the 13th cent. or before.

Loans from individual money-lenders to individual borrowers e.g. in Somaganda's insc. have been referred to loans from individual to assembly were not uncommon. In the reign of Rajaraja I, the sabha of Vaduturai owed money to one Kaikkola on a promissory note (Kaiyeluttodai). When for some reason the entire property of Kaikkolan including his loan assets was attached by the state, the assembly was asked to repay the loan; it then assigned land to temple to borrow money from it to pay the king (105 of 1925). The assembly of Kudamukku received 100 Kasu from a native of Marudam

31. A.C. Ghosh, Law of Endow., p. 224.

to utilise them in repairing the damages to irrigation channels caused by the Kaveri floods. The interest at the high rate of 1 kalam per Kasu was paid towards the services in a temple (214 of 1911).

While some Brahmins stood sureties for unpaid dues (treated as debt to king), mahajanas stood witnesses in some endowment records.[32] Witnesses were also named in inscribed mortgages (cf. Jaunpur Br. Insc. Rewa Pls.). A comparison of capital outlay may not be out of place. Whereas 100 Kasu were required to feed 10 Sivayogins on 24 days in a year (i e. 250 Sivayogins at a time—no. 28 of S.I.I. II) from the income, 65 kal of gold was deposited to feed 1 Sivayogin throughout the year (i.e. 365 Sivayogins at a time) in the 5th yr. of Aditya II (225 of 1911). 9 dra. per month on an endowment (or 108 dra) all the year round were required in Gujerat to feed a Brahmin student. A.K. Majumdar (p. 251) relates this to daily wage, but as Basham[33] points out, much depends on the weight and metal of a coin. Whereas 15 kal. were sufficient for the supply of 1 ulokku of oil daily in Rajaraja's 3rd yr. (262 of 1910, 295 of 1906), 30 kal. were necessary for the same performance in the 4th yr. of Parakesari (268 of 1910) and in the 31st yr. of Parantaka I (E.I. V. 26, p. 230). While criticising Pran Nath's view that the capital outlay for feeding a monk in the south was higher than in the north, Altekar (p. 387) holds that it was 8-16 kal. in the south. The instance of 85 kal. must balance his statement. As he himself observes, no precise comparison is possible and no reliance can be put on a particular ratio of dinara and Kalanju. From the reduced quantity of ghee as daily interest (1 ulakku and 1 alakku) for the capital of 20 kal. shown on his Table XV, compared to 1 uri daily for the same capital in earlier times. Pran Nath (p. 99) holds that there had been both a reduction in the rate of interest and a rise in the price of ghee from the 9th to the 11th cent.

32. E.I. XXV. 56.

33. Puri Ins.

The price of paddy is stated to be $2^3/_4$ kalam per Kasu in prices. It was 4 kalam per Kasu in Tiruvallam Ins. of Adhirajendra. If the rates of interest on two deposits in the same record from Tanjore—one in grain and the other in money, are taken to be the same, i.e. to say if 3 kuruni are taken to be equivalent to $^1/_3$ Kasu which is the interest on 1 Kasu therein the price of paddy in the time of Rajaraja and Rajendra may be taken to be 24 kuruni or 2 kalam (by the 8 nali or 12 kuruni measure) per Kasu. The exchange value of a Kasu is thus seen to be abnormally low and the price of paddy too high. In a developed agrarian economy, paddy is not expected to have sold so dear, except because campaigns of the empire-builders and calamities strained the economy much. In no. 151 of S.I I. XIII, 200 kal. were equivalent to 3000 kalam of paddy, i.e. to say 1 kal. fetched 15 kalam (and 1 Kasu sometimes 7½ kalam). In another record, 60 kal. were equivalent to ?25 Kadi of paddy, i.e. to say 1 kal = $3^2/_3$ Kadi (V.R.p. 40 no. 80). The price of land was quoted as 2000 kuli for 50 Kasu in S.I.I. III no 54 and 800 kuli for 64 Kasu (= $22^3/_4$ kal.) in another record (5 of 1890). In scill another (509 of 1912), 90 Kasu (of 3/4 kal. of gold each) bought 4 velis of land. Land prices varied depending on the nature of land (nanjai =wet, punjai = dry), yield and possibly also category of tenancy. The exchange rate 1 Kasu = 3 ewes is mentioned in no. 6, 63 etc., S.I.I. II ; it was 1 Kasu = 4 ewes in 1. 17-18 in no. 95 ib. No. 37 ib. shows 1 Kasu = 1200 plantains. Camphor was 2½ karanju per Kasu in no. 9 and 3 karanju in no. 27 ib. In the north if the prices in Bhaskara's[34] sums leave any indication, 1 pala of camphor could be had for 2 niskas, 1 pala of sandalwood for $^1/_8$ dra and $^1/_2$ pala of aloc-wood for $^1/_8$ dra. ; $1^1/_8$ khari of rice cost 2 dra., the best silk-scarf (8 by 8 cubits) cost 100 niskas and a female slave of 16 years 32 niskas.[35]

34. Chron List of Insc. from Pudukottai St.—No. 499.

35. Nadol Insc., E.I. XI 37, IX. 1.

In a situation like this marked with divergent prices, diverse measures, utter currency confusion[36] and innumerable rates of interest it is the bankers, grain dealers and shroffs who reign supreme and the common man ever falls a prey to their chicanery and sinks into indebtedness.

36. Review of Majumdar, Chalukyas of Gujerat, in J.E.S.H.O. Vol. I.

Select Bibliography

ORIGINAL SOURCES

Literary

Atharva Veda, Ed. Roth and Whitney (Berlin, 1855) Eng. Tr. Griffith, I-II (Benares 1895-6) Tr. and Notes Whitney (H.O.S. 1905) Vols. VII-VIII Revised by Lanman.

Rgveda, Ed. Max Muller, I-IV, (Lond. 1849-74). Eng. Tr. H.H. Wilson I-VI (Lond. 1850-88) Oldenberg, S.B.E. Vol. 46, Ger. Tr. Geldner, (H.O.S. 33-35, 1951),

Aitareya Brahmana, Ed. Samasrami (B. I. Cal. 1895-1906), M. Haug. Tr. Keith H.O.S. 25 (Cam. 1920).

Kathaka Samhita, Ed. Schroeder, (Leipzig 1911).

Kausika Sutra, Ed. Bloomfield (New Haven 1889).

Kausitaki Brahmana, Ed. Cowell, (Cal. 1861) Tr. Keith (H.O.S. 25).

Gopatha Brahmana, Ed. Mitra and Vidyabhusana (Cal. 1872).

Gobhila Grhya Sutra, Ed. Tarkalankara (Cal. 1908).

Chhandogya Brahmana, Ed. D.M. Bhattacharya (Cal. 1958).

Taittiriya Aranyaka, Ed. Mitra (Cal. 1872).

Taittiriya Brahmana, Ed. Mitra (Cal. 1855-70).

Taittiriya Samhita, Ed. Cowell and Others (Cal. 1860-99) Tr. Keith, H.O.S.

Nirukta, Ed. Rajavada (Poona 1921-26), Samasrami I-IV (Cal. 1882-91).

Panchavimsa Brahman, Ed. Vedanta Vagisa (Cal. 1874).

Maitrayani Samhita, Ed. Schroeden (Leipzig 1886).

Vajasaneyi Samhita, Ed. Weber (Berlin 1852),

Samaveda, Ed. Tr. Benfey (Leizig 1848).

Satapatha Brahmana, Ed. Weber (Lond. 1885), Tr. Eggeling, S.B.E. 12, 25, 41, 43, 45 (Oxford 1882-1900).

Sankhayano Aranyaka, Friedlander, I-II (1900), Cowell, III-VI (1861), Keith VII-XV (1909).

Smrti Texts with Comm.

Apastamba Dharma Sutra, Ed. Buhler (Bom. 1892) Tr. Do. S.B.E. II (1879).

Katyayana Smrtisaroddhara, Ed. Tr., P.V. Kane, Bom. 1933.

Gautama Dharma Sutra, Ed. Gokhale (A.S.S. 1910) with Comm. of Haradatta; Srinivasacharya with Comm. of Maskari (1917) Tr. Buhler, S.B.E. II.

Narada Smrti, Ed. Jolly (Cal. 1885) Tr. S.B.E. 33 (1889).

Naradiya Manu, Ed. K.S. Sastri Trivandrum (1929).

Prasara Smrti, Ed. Tarkalankara (Cal. 1892), Ed. Islampurkar with Madhava's Comm. (Bom. 1906).

Brhaspati Smrti, Ed. Aiyangar (Baroda 1941).

Baudhayana Dharma Sutra, Ed. A.C. Sastri (Benares 1934) Tr. S.B.E. 14 (1882).

Manu Smrti, Ed. Mandlik (Bom. 1886), G.N. Jha (Cal. 1939) with Comm. of Medhatithi. Tr. Buhler S.B.E. 25 (1886).

Yajnavalkya Smrti, Ed. with Apararka's Com. in Anandasram, (No. 46) with Mitaksra, Pansikar (Bom. 1909) with Visvarupa's comm. T.S. Sastri (Triv. 1922) with Balambhatti on Mitaksara—ed. Parvatiya (Benares 1914).

Basistha Dharmasastra, Ed. Buhler (Bom. 1883) Tr. S.B.E. 14, (1882),

Visnu Smrti, Ed. Jolly (Cal. 1881) Tr. S.B.E. 7.

Dharmakosa, D.S. Joshi (Wai 1937-53).

Smrtisamgraha—anonymous.

Early Grammar, Epic and Puranas

Panini—Astadhyayi, Ed. and Tr. S.C. Basu, 2 Vols. Delhi, 1962.

Patanjali—Mahabhasya, Ed. Kielhorn, 3 Vols, Bom. 1880-5.

Mahabharata—Edited by Kinjawadekar with comm. of Nilakantha (Poona, 1929-33) Ed. B.I., Cal. 1834-39, Eng. Tr. by K.M. Ganguly, Cal. 1926-32.

Ramayana—Ed. Raghu Vira, Lahore 1938; Tr. Griffith, Benares, 1950.

Agni Purana—Ed. R. Mitra, Cal. 1873-79, Tr. by M.N. Dutt, Cal. 1901.

Garuda Purana—Ed. Bombay, 1906, Tr. by M.N. Dutt, Cal. 1906.

Padma Purana —Ed. Mandlik Ananda, Poona 1905.

Matsya Purana Ed. Poona, 1907, Tr. S.B.H. (2 Vols.), 1916-17.

Visnudharmottara Purana —Bombay 1912.

Works on Polity

Kamandaka-Nitisara—Ed. Mitra, Cal. 1884.

Kautilya-Arthasastra—Ed. Shamasastri, Mysore, 1919, Tr. Do. 1929. Ed. T.G. Sastri, Triv. 1925, Ed. Venkatanathachariya, Mysore, 1960, Ed. Basak, Cal. 1970.

Sukraniti—Ed. Oppert, Mad, 1882. Tr. B.K. Sarkar, Allahabad, 192 .

Buddhist and Jain Texts

Anguttara Nikaya—Ed. R. Morris & E. Hardy, London, 1900, Eng. Tr. by F.L. Woodward & E.M. Hare, Lond., 1932-36.

Digha Nikaya—Ed. T.W. Rhys Davids & J.E. Carpenter, 3 Vols., P.T.S. Lond. 1890, 1903, 1911. Eng. Tr. by T.W. Rhys Davids, 3 Vols., Lond., 1899, 1910 & 1921.

Divyavadana—Ed. Cowell and Neill, Cam. 1886.

Itivuttaka—Ed. E. Windisch, PTS, London, 1889.

Jatakas—Ed. V. Fausboll, 6 Vols., Lond. 1887-97. Eng. Tr. by E.B. Cowell, 6 Vols., Cambridge 1895-1913. Excerpts Tr. Burlingame Vol. 7 (Index).

Majjhima Nikaya—Ed. Trenckner, London 1880. Tr. Rhys Davids, SBE. Oxford, 1890-94.

Mulasarvastivada Vinaya—Gilgit Manuscripts, Ed. Dr. N. Dutta.

Saddharmapundarika—Ed. Bib. Bud. St. Peters, Tr. S.B.E. 21.

Samyutta Nikaya—Ed. by Leon Freer, RTS, London, 1884-98. Eng. Tr. by Mrs. Davids & F.L. Woodward, PTS, Lond. 1917-30.

Saratthappkasani—Ed. Woodward.

Sutta Nipata—Ed. by D. Anderson & H. Smith, PTS, Lond. 1913.

Thera-gatha—Ed. Oldenberg. PTS, London, 1883. Tr. Mrs. Rhys Davids.

Theri-gatha—Ed. Pischel, PTS, London 1883, Tr. Mrs. Rhys Davids, PTS, London, 1909.

Vinaya Pitaka—Ed. Oldenberg, PTS, London, 1879-83, Tr. Rhys Davids and Oldenberg, SBE, Oxford, 1881-85.

Acharanga Sutra—Ed. Schubring, Tr. S.B.E. 22.

Antagadadasao—Ed. Bombay, 1920, Tr.L.D. Barnett (Lond. 1907).

Avasyaka tika—Haribhadra.

Avasyaka churni—Jinadasa Gani.

Jambudvipa pannatti—Comm. Santichandra.

Kalpasutra (Brhat Kalpasutrea)—Ed. Schubring. Leipzig, 1905; cf. Bhadrabahu Ed. Jacobi. Leipzig, 1879. Tr. H. Jacobi SBE. Oxford, 1892; Ed. Malayagiri and Kseemakirti.

Other Skt. Texts with Prakrit, Tamil and Bens. Texts

Anandabhatta—Vallalacharita Ed. H.P. Sastri, Cal. 1904.

Aryabhatta—Ed. Kern, Leiden, 1874 Cf. Jaye, J.P. A.S.B. 1908.

Bhaskara-Lilavati—Ed. D. Sarma (Mithila) Bijaganita, Ed. A. Jha, Tr. Colebrooke, Algebra, 1817.

Bhuvanadeva—Aparajitaprchchha Ed. Mankad, G.O.S. 115.

Brahmagupta-Brahmasphuta-siddhanta—Ed. R.S. Sharma, Tr. Colebrooke, Algebra, 1817.

Damodara Kuttanimatam—Ed. M. Kaul, Tr. Mathers.

Damodara Uktivyaktiprakarana—Ed. J.V. Muni.

Gopalabhatta-Vallala Charita—Ed. Harischandra Kaviratna 1889.

Hala-Gatha Saptasati—Ed. R.G. Basak.

Harsa-Naisadhiya Ed. P.C. Pandir.

Hemachandra—Dvyasraya Kavya with Comm. of A. Gani Ed. Kathavate.

Ilango-Silappadilaram—Ed. S. Aiyar, Tr. Dikshitar.

Isvaradatta and others—Chaturbhani Ed. Kavi and Ramnath Patna, 1922.

Jalhana-Sukti—(Subhasita) Muktavali (G.O.S. 82).

Jyotisatattvavaridhi—N. Vidyanidhi.

Kalhana-Rajatarangini—Ed. D. Prasad, Ed. Tr. Stein.

Ksemendra-Lokaprakasa—Ed. J. Zadoo, Samaya Matrka Ed. Prasad and Parab, Tr. Mathers Brhat Kathamanjari.

Lekhapaddhati—Ed. Dalal and Shrigodenkar.

Mahasuphasitasamgraha—Ed. Sternbach.

Mahavira-Ganitasara—Ed. Tr. M. Rangaraja, Mad. 1912.

Merutunga-Prabandhachintamani—Ed. J.V. Muni Tr. Tawney.

Maimansimha Gitika—Ed. D.C. Sen.

Muhurttachintamani—Ramacharya.

Narayana-Hitopadesa—Ed. Peterson, 1883.

Paditrupatty—Ed. S. Aiyar Tr. 'Ten Idylls', Chelliyah.

Puratana Prabandha Samgraha—Ed. J.V. Muni. Singji Jain Series.

Rajasekhara-Kavyamimamsa—Ed. Dalal and Sastri, Baroda, 1934.

Rajasekhara-Prabandhakosa.

Sakatayana-Sabdanusasana—Bombay 1907.

Samalabhat-Vidyavilasini.

Sattanar-Manimekalai—Ed. Aiyar.

Siddharsi-Upamitibhava—Prapancha katha Ed. Peterson and Jacobi.

Somadeva-Yasastilaka—Ed. Sivadatla and Parab, Bombay, 1903.

Somadeva-Kathasaritsagara—Ed. Prasad and Parab. Tr. Tawney.

Somesvara-Manasollasa—Ed. Shrigondekar.

Sripati-Ganitatilaka—G.O.S. no. 78.

Tiruvalluvar—Kurel, Tr. Poplay.

Tolkappiyar—Tolkappiyam.

Varahamihira—Brhajjataka Ed. S. Jha.

Vidyapati—Likhanavali, Bihar Rastrabhasa Parisad.

Visnusarman-Panchatantra—Ed. Parab, Ed. Hertal, Tr. Ryder.

Lexicons

Amarakosa with Comm. of Ksirasvamin,

Hatayudhakosa.

Vachaspatyam.

Vaijayanti.

Inscriptions

Annual Reports on Epigraphy, Madras (1890-1945) A.R.E. (ref. e.g. 5 of 1890) Delhi (1945).

Annual Reports of the Mysore Archaeological Dept. (Bangalore) A.R. Mys. Arch. Dept.

Archaeological Survey of Western India Reports—A.S.W.I.

Corpus Inscriptionum Indicarum Vol. III ed. Fleet, Vol. IV ed. Mirashi. C.I,L.

Chronological List of Inscriptions of the Pudukottai State, 1929—Chron. List etc.

Epigraphica Carnatica—Vols. E.C.

Epigraphia Indica—Vols. E.I.

Historical Inscriptions of Southern India—Sewell and Others.

Indian antiquary—Vols. I.A.

Inscriptions of the Madras Presidency, Vols. I-II, V. Rangacharya, 1919—V.R.

Karnataka Inscriptions—Vols. I-II, ed. Panchamukhi, 1941, 1951—K.I.

Select Inscriptions—Ed. D.C. Sircar, Cal. 1965, 2nd edn.—S.I.

South Indian Inscriptions—Vols. I-XVIII, Madras (1890)—S.I.L.

Travancore Archaeological Series—Trav. Arch. Se.

Coins

Altekar—Catalogue of the Gupta Gold Coins in the Bayana Board.

Smith—Catalogue of the Coins in the Indian Museum.

SECONDARY SOURCES

Adhya, G.L.—Early Indian Economics.

Agarwala—India as known to Panini.

Aiyar—Cera kings of the Sangam period.

Altekar—Position of Women.

———The Rastrakutas and their times (Poona 1934).

Appadorai—Economic conditions in Southern India, Vols. I-II, Madras, 1936.

Apte—Social and Religious Life in the Grhasutras.

Aristotle—Politics—Tr. Jowett.

Arokiaswami—The Kongu Country.

Banerjee, N.C.—Economic Life and Progress in Ancient India, Vol. I, Cal. 1945.

Barnett, L.D.—Antiquities of India, Lond. 1913.

Basham, A.L.—The Wonder that was India.

———Studies in Indian History, Lond. 1953.

Beal—Siyuki : Buddhist Records of the Western World, ? Vols, London, 1884.

Beneviste, E.—Indo-European Language and Society.

Bhandarkar, D.R.—Carmichael Lectures—I, II.

Bhandarkar, R.G.—Early History of Dekkan.

Bongard-Levin—Studies in Ancient India and Central Asia.

Bose, A.N.—Social and Rural Economy of Northern India, Vols. I & II, Cal. 1942-5.

Bose, N.S.—History of the Chandellas of Jetakabhukti, Cal. 1956.

Chakravarti, S.—Study of Ancient Indian Numismatics.

Chatterji, B.—Kushana State and Indian Society.

Chatterji, H.C.—Law of Dept. in Ancient India, Sanskrit College, Cal. 1971.

Chatterji, S.K.—Social Life in Ancient India, Cal. 1965.

Chaudhuri, P.C.—History of Civilisation of the People of Assam.

Colebrooke—Algebra with Arithmetic and Mensuration from the Sanskrit of Brahmagupta and Bhaskara.

Coomaraswamy, A.—Indian Craftsman.

Das, A.C.—Rg Vedic Culture.

——Rg Vedic India.

Das, D.R.—Economic History of Deccan.

Das, S.R.—Archaeological Discoveries from Murshidabad.

Das, S.K.—Economic Life of Ancient India, Cal. 1925.

Das, R.M.—Women in Manusmrti.

Deo, S.B.—Jain Monastic Jurisprudence.

Derrett—The Hoysalas, Oxford 1957.

——Religion, Law and State in India.

Desai, P.B.—Jainism in South India.

Deshpande—Indological Papers, Vol. I.

Driver and Miles—The Babylonian Laws.

Durant, W.—Our Oriental Heritage.

Dutt, A.—Perspectives of Economic Development.

Dutt, A.N.—Early History of the Spread of Buddhism and the Buddhist Schools.

Dutt, R.C.—History of Civilisation in Ancient India, Vols. I, II, London, 1893.

Dehejia, Vidya—Early Buddhist Rock Temples.

Elliot and Dowson—History of India as told by its own Historians.

Fick, R.—The Social Organisation in North East India in Buddha's Times, Tr. by S.K. Maitra, Cal. 1920.

Ganguli, B.N.—Readings in Indian Economic History, Delhi, 1961. Delhi School of Economics.

Ganguly, D.C.—History of the Paramara Dynasty.

Ghosal, U.N.—History of Hindu Public Life.

——Studies in Indian History and Culture.

Ghosh, A.—City in Early Historical India.

Gyani, S.D.—Agni Purana—a Study.

Gopal, L.—Economic Life of N. India, Delhi, 1965.

Gopal, M.—Mauryan Public Finance.

Gopalachari—Early History of Andhra Country.

Gour—The History and Law of Interest.

Gururajachar—Aspects of Economic and Social Life in Karnataka.

Haney—History of Economic Thought, Macmillan, 1917.

Hazra, R.C.—Studies in Puranic Records.

Hillebrandt—Vedische Mythologie.

Hirth & Rockhill—Chau-Ju-Kua.

Jain, J.C.—Life in Ancient India as depicted in Jain Canons (Bomb. 1947).

Jolly—Recht und Sitte, 1896, Tr. by B.K. Ghosh, Cal. 1928.

Kaegi—The Rg Veda.

Kane, P.V.—History of Dharma Sastra, Vol. II, Part I, Poona 1941, Do, Vol. III, 1946.

Keith—History of Sanskrit Literature.

Keith and Macdonell—Vedic Index, Vols. I, II.

Kosambi, D.D.—Myth and Reality.

——Culture and Civilisation of Ancient India, Delhi, 1970.

Krader—Ethnological Notes of Karl Marx.

Law, B.C.—India as described in Early Texts of Buddhism and Jainism.

McCrindle—Ancient India as described by Megasthenes and Arrian.

Macdonell—Vedic Mythology.

Mahalingam—Kanchipuram in South Indian History.

Maity, S.K.—Economic Life of Northern India in the Gupta Period, Cal. 1957.

Majumdar, A.K.—Chalukyas of Gujarat, Bombay, 1966.

Majumdar, M.R.—Cultural History of Gujarat.

Majumdar, R.C.—Corporate Life in Ancient India.

——History of Bengal, Vol. I, Dacca, 1943.

——ed. Vidyabhuvan Series, Bombay (1951-57).

——(i) The Vedic Age.
(ii) The Age of Imperial Unity.
(iii) The Classical Age.
(iv) The Age of Imperial Kanauj.
(v) The Struggle for Empire.

Mauss, M.—The Gift.

Mazumdar, B.P.—Socio-Economic History of Northern India, Cal. 1960.

Mehta, R.L.—Pre-Buddhist India.

Minakshi, C.—Administrative and Social Life under the Pallavas.

Minakshi Sundaram, T.P.—History of Tamil Language.

Mitra, B.C.—Letters of Credit.

Mohahan—Early History of Bengal, Oxford, 1925.

Morton—A Collection of Proverbs.

Mukherji, B.N.—Nana on Lien.

——Economic Factors in Kushana History.

Muller—Ancient Sanskrit Literature.

——Ed. Sacred Books of the East.

Nainar—Arab Geographers' Knowledge of Southern India.

Nelson—The Idea of Usury.

Niyogi, P.—Economic History of Northern India, Cal. 1962.

Niyogi, R.—History of Gahadavala Dynasty.

Oldenberg—Die Religion des Veda.

Percival—Tamil Proverbs.

Pirenne, H.—Economic and Social History of Medieval Europe.

Pischel—Vedische Studien.

Pran Nath—A Study in the Economic Condition of Ancient India, London, 1929.

Puri, B.N.—India in the days of Patanjali, Bom. 1957.

——The History of the Gurjara-Pratiharas, Bomb. 1957.

Ragozin—Vedic India.

Ramgopal—India of Vedic Kalpasutras.

Rapsion, E.J.—Cambridge History of India, Vol. I, 1922.

Roy, H.C.—Dynastic History of Northern India, 2 Vols., Calcutta, 1931, 1936.

Ray, N.R.—Bangalir Itihas Adiparva, Cal. B.S. 1956.

Renaudot—Ancient Accounts of India and China by two Muhammadan Travellers (Lond. 1933).

Rhys Davids, T.W.—Buddhist India, Lond. 1903.

Sachao—Alberuni's India, 2 Vols. London, 1910.

Saletore—Early Indian Economic History.

Samaddar, J.N.—The Economic Condition of Ancient India, C.U. 1922.

Sarkar, B.K.—The Positive Background of Hindu Sociology, Allahabad, 1914, S.B.H.—Vol. XXV.

Sastri, K.A.N.—Comprehensive History of India, Vol. II, Pub. Indian History Congress, 1957.

——The Colas, Madras, 1955.

——History of South India, Oxford Univ. Press, 1955.

Schoff, W.A.—The Periplus of the Erythrean Sea. London, 1912.

Sen, B.C.—Studies in the Buddhist Jatakas, Cal. 1974.

——Economics in the Kautilya, Sanskrit College, Cal. 1967.

——Some Historical Aspects of the Inscriptions of Bengal, Cal. 1942.

Sharma, D.—Early Chauhan Dynasties, 1959.

Sharma, G.R.—Exacavations at Kausambi (1957-59).

Sharma, R.S.—Light on early Indian Society and Economy, 1966.

——Indian Feudalism.

——The Sudras in Ancient India.

Sircar, D.C.—Social Life in Ancient India (ed.), C.U. 1971.

——Studies in Religious Life in Ancient India.

——Epigraphic Glossary.

Smith, Adam—Wealth of Nations.

Srivastava—Trade and Commerce in Ancient India.

Stein, Otto—Jinist Studies.

Sternbach—Juridical Studies in Ancient Indian Law, 2 Vols. Delhi, 1965-67.

Takasusu, T.—Record of the Buddhistic Religion as practised in India and the Malay Archipelago, Oxford, 1896.

Tawney, R.H.—Religion and Rise of Capitalism, Middles, 1926.

Thakur, U.—History of Mithila, Darbhanga, 1956.

Thapar, R.—History of India, Vol. I.

Toynbe—A Study of History, Oxford, 1933-39.

Vaidya, C.V.—Epic India.

Varma, V.P.—Early Buddhism and its Origin.

Vedam, Mitra—India of Dharma Sutras.

Birji, K.N.—Ancient History of Saurastra.

Weber, Max.—The Religion of India.

——Sociology of Religion.

——The City.

Zimmer—Altendisches Laben.

Commemoration and Felicitation Volumes

A.N. Jha—Felicitation Volume.

Asutosh Commemoration Volume.

B.C. Law Vol. Parts I and II.

Das Capital Centenary Volume.

K.B. Pathak Commemoration Volume.

Mirashi Felicitation Volume.

S.C. Sarkar Felicitation Volume.

Concordance & Bibliographies

Bloomfield—Vedic Concordance

C.L. Jain—Jain Bibliography.

Woodward—Pali Tripitaka Concordance.

Vedic Bibliography, Vols. I-III—International Biblio. of Historical Sciences.

Velankar—Jinaratnakosa (Poona).

Encyclopaedias

Encyclopaedia of Social Sciences.

The Universal Encyclopaedia of Mathematics.

Dictionaries

Apte—Practical Skt-Eng. Dictionary.

Buddhist Hybrid Skt. Grammar and Dictionary.

Monier-Williams—Skt.-Eng. Dictionary.

St. Petersberg Dictionary.

Wilson—Glossary.

Journals

Ancient India—Anc. India.

Anekant (Hindi).

Annals of the Bhandarkar (Oriental Research) Institute—A.B.O.R.I.

Aryasastra (Skt. Texts with Bengali Tr. Sponsored by Sri Sitaramadasa Onkaranatha).

Asiatic Researches—As. Res.

Bulletin of the School of Oriental and African Studies—Bull. School etc.

Current Science.

Indian Advocate.

Indian Culture—I.C.

Indian Economic and Social History Review—I.E.S.H.R.

Indian Journal of Social Work—I.J.S.W.

Indian Studies Past and Present—I.S.P.P.

International Congress of Orientalists—Int. Con. Orient.

Journal of Ancient Indian History (C.U.—J.A.I.H.

Journal of American Oriental Society, J.A.O.S.

Journal of Asian Studies—J.A.S.

Journal of Bihar and Orissa Research Society—J.B.O.R.S.

Journal of Bombay Branch of Royal Asiatic Society—J.B.B.R.A.S.

Journal of the Dept. of Letters, (C.U.)—J.D.L.

Journal of Economic History—J.E.H.

Journal of Economic and Social History of the Orient—J.E.S.H.O.

Journal of Indian History—J.I.H.

Journal of Mysore University—J.M.U.

Journal of the Numismatic Society of India—J.N.S.I.

Journal and Proceedings of the Asiatic Society of Bengal—J.P.A.S.B.

Journal of the United Provinces Historical Society—J.U.P.H.S.

Memoirs, Asiatic Society of Bengal—M.A.S.B.

Madhya Bharati.

Proceedings, Indian History Congress—P.I.H.C.

Quarterly Journal of Mythic Society—Q.J.M.S.

Vishveshvarananda Indological Journal—Vish. Indol. J.

Zeitchrift fur Vergleichende Rechtswissenschaft—Z.V.R.

Index